WINNING

THE BATTLE TO BELONG

The Key Ingredient to
Reaching College Students

BRIAN SMITH SR.

© 2023 by Brian Smith Sr.

Published in Phoenix, Arizona by Hope Church Movement

ISBN 979-8-218-19973-9

All scripture quotations, unless otherwise indicated, are taken from the New American Standard Bible. The Lockman Foundation, 1995.

Scripture quotations identified NLT are from the Holy Bible, New Living Translation. Tyndale House Publishers, 1996.

Names and some details in anecdotes and stories have been changed to protect the identities of the persons involved.

To my wife, my family, and the Hope Church family.

Wendy, after my decision to follow Jesus, marrying you was the best decision I've ever made.

Brian Jr., Caleb, and Noah, I'm so proud of the men you've become and the impact you're each having.

Hope Church, it's an honor to pastor you as we help the next generation find and follow Jesus, walk in freedom and live on mission.

"Change the campus, change the world."

- Dr. Rice Broocks

WHAT PEOPLE ARE SAYING

"There's not a timelier book than Brian Smith's *Winning the Battle to Belong*. Our greatest mission field is not in a far-away place. Our greatest mission field is the next generation! This seminal book offers both current strategies as well as renewing tried-and-true principles we have long forgotten. Brian's many years of successful engagement in college ministry adds great credibility, proven strategy, and life-changing testimonies. His book leaves us a pathway to follow…and follow, we must!"

Dr. Wayne Cordeiro
Author and Founding Pastor of New Hope Christian Fellowship in Honolulu, HI

"It's difficult to overstate the importance of what Brian is communicating in this book. If you care about the spiritual state of America, the university campus should be at the top of your list of concerns. *Winning the Battle to Belong* offers solutions to the challenge of reaching students with the gospel."

Dr. Rice Broocks
Best-selling author of God's Not Dead; Cofounder of Every Nation Churches & Ministries; Senior Minister of Bethel World Outreach in Nashville, TN

"Brian and Wendy have pioneered an approach to reaching college students that is working. They have developed a strategy that we would be wise to embrace and support. I highly recommend *Winning the Battle to Belong* to anyone who wants to learn how to reach the upcoming generations with the gospel. In my 40 years of working in higher education, I've never seen anyone do collegiate-ministry better than Hope Church."

Ray Jensen
Former Associate Vice President at Arizona State University;
President of Life Relaunch

"As a mom, I nervously sent my son off to college hoping he would make the right choices. I'm grateful and blessed that my son Shawn met a campus minister on his first day of college. What Pastor Brian, his wife Wendy and their incredible team do on our college campuses is nothing short of amazing. Their love for God and sharing the gospel with college students changed my son's life and thousands of others. Because of Hope, my son, who sadly passed away at 20 years old, is wrapped in God's arms now and I know I will see him again someday. Also, the friendships he made through Hope carry on to this day and they stay in touch with me and our family. I am forever grateful to the mission this church is on for our children's future."

Jill Sennewald
Parent of Student

"This is a RIGHT NOW book, written at the RIGHT TIME by the RIGHT GUY! I have known Brian for several years, and my goodness, his personal story is compelling but it is also a testimony and a template for why the Body of Christ must engage our college campuses. Every pastor and next gen pastor needs to read this book, and then let the Holy Spirit lead them into how to engage the college students living near them in their community. The next generation is at stake. We can't delay on this! We have to engage in the Battle to Belong!"

Matt Keller

Founding and Lead Pastor of Next Level Church in Fort Myers, FL; Founder of Next Level Relational Network of Churches

"No one understands the new freshmen on a college campus more than Brian Smith. Taken from his own collegiate experience, along with decades of creative and relational outreach to incoming students, you'll gain fresh vision and practical ideas to win the Battle to Belong on your campus. You and your team immerse yourself with these principles, then come up with your own strategic plan to reach hundreds of students each fall with the gospel of Jesus Christ. Why? Reach the campus, reach the world!"

Dr. Steve Shadrach

Global Ambassador, Center for Mission Mobilization; Founder of Student Mobilization; Cofounder of The Traveling Team; Author and Former Mobilization Director for the U.S. Center for World Mission

"Our culture is longing for relationships because everyone has a deep desire to belong. This book captures the incredible strategy that God has given Hope Church Movement to reach the next generation of students on college campuses. If you're a parent, ministry leader or simply have a heart for college students, I highly recommend this book for you and everyone you know."

Dr. Don Wilson

Founding Pastor of Christ's Church of the Valley in Peoria, AZ; President of Accelerate Group

"Wow! Simple, yet profound, and it works! This is the way to be a collegiate-focused church."

Al Ells

President of Leaders that Last

"I've known Brian and Wendy for nearly two decades. We've worked closely in ministry, and I've had the pleasure of serving on the Advisory Board of Hope Church. Brian and Wendy's ministry to college students is extraordinary. We've experienced it personally in their dynamic weekend services and phenomenal special events. It's time for the world of campus ministries to hear their story in this book. It will inspire you and give you a bundle of creative ideas for your ministry."

Dr. Gary Kinnaman

Retired Megachurch Pastor; Author & Chairman of the Governor's Council on Faith and Community

"This book can change the world, if taken seriously. Brian Smith knows what he's talking about. He's done it for more than 30 years, and I've experienced up close the fruit of his ministry, and it's real – college students passionate and zealous about reaching the lost, with a joy and a warm camaraderie that's infectious. This is a lean book, without fluff, and Brian lays out practical steps to reaching college students. You'll get blessed, motivated as well as get a clear road map for how to approach the college campus of today. This might be the best, most accessible and galvanizing book on campus ministry."

Ed Kang
Pastor of Gracepoint Ministries

"I have observed Brian Smith from his teenage years and rejoice at how God is working through him to reach thousands of college students for Christ. In Winning the Battle to Belong, Brian issues an impassioned plea to reach out to students within the first critical days after they arrive on campus. And he provides an effective strategy on how to welcome them into the family of God. Writing from his own experience as a student and from his 30+ years of being a pastor to students, Brian shares his conviction that most college students are "harassed and helpless, like sheep without a shepherd" (Matt 9:36). These students are in danger of being swept away by the "rapid river of secular campus culture." However, Brian also communicates a message of hope. He reminds his readers that many of these students are open to being introduced to the Good Shepherd and to experiencing radically transformed lives as they follow Him."

Rick Efird
Director of Church Partnerships at Phoenix Seminary

"The college campus is the best place to reach a person for Christ. The first days that a student steps onto campus is the best time to reach them! Why? People tend to come to Christ in trouble and transition, and this is often the first major transition in life. Also, a college campus is a "recruitment culture" where every club and organization is actively recruiting students. In *Winning the Battle to Belong,* Brian Smith gives the inspiration and application needed to maximize your impact for the gospel on campus. Read it, discuss it with your team and make your own customized plan to reach as many students as possible for the glory of God!"

Paul Worcester
National Collegiate Director North American Mission Board; Author of The Fuel and The Flame: Ignite Your Life and Your Campus for Jesus Christ

"I have had the good fortune of knowing Brian and Wendy Smith for over 25 years. In *Winning the Battle to Belong*, Brian skillfully diagnoses and demonstrates the universal longings that this generation of college students have. Finding "one's purpose" and "having a sense of belonging" are pressing issues in a postmodern, relativistic world. Many books can readily identify the problems, but Pastor Brian Smith has successfully introduced a solution that has been and continues to equip young Christians, impacting thousands of lives across the country. *Winning the Battle to Belong* is a must read for anyone who is concerned about spreading the gospel message and making disciples."

Dr. Ken Dew
Every Nation Ministry; Equipping Evangelist, Apologist & Author

"I met Pastor Brian many years ago, when he showed up at one of my comedy shows and told me he wanted to use comedy to reach the college crowd. Well, he had me at 'hello.' His type of crazy fit my wheelhouse very well. Over the years, I've been able to watch and help Hope Church do its outreach, and I can tell you Pastor Brian is dedicated to reaching university students for Christ. I hope and pray that we can get many more versions of Hope Church, and other churches like it, to truly make a change on the college campus. It's time for the church to make an all out assault for the next generation, and this book tells us how. It's the recipe for the secret sauce of how to reach college students."

Ron Pearson
Actor and Comedian

"Pastor Brian Smith is on an urgent and much needed mission. Inspired by Jesus and His Great Commission to go and reach the lost, he shares the importance of being intentional and proactive about living out this great calling in *Winning the Battle to Belong*. I have had the blessing of knowing Brian and Wendy for many years now, and I've been inspired by their commitment and passion for reaching the hearts of college students. I have seen firsthand how they live out the principles he shares in his book and the fruits that have come from them taking action. I have witnessed so many college students' lives changed as they've found a new place to belong! Readers will be convicted, encouraged, and equipped to reach college students in a real and transformative way for the sake of the gospel!"

Kylie Bisutti

Author of I'm No Angel: From Victoria's Secret Model to Role Model

"God gives all of us a passion to make a difference in our broken world, and it is without a doubt that he has given my friend Brian Smith a passion for college age young adults. We are seeing a generation of young people searching for value and meaning; wrestling with record levels of anxiety and wondering if anyone sees them. In the midst of this crisis, God has given Brian a clear vision of hope, healing, and a reminder that students are not alone. If you care about bringing hope to this generation, this book is for you."

Dan Steffen

Senior Pastor of Pure Heart Church in Glendale, AZ

"If our leaders of tomorrow come from today's universities, then the need to introduce the gospel to the students and staff at universities is urgent. We need a way to engage with students that works. In this book, Pastor Brian Smith lays out a method for bringing the gospel to college students that is effective and fun. I know it works because I've seen it work with my own eyes. Shortly after my son started his freshman year at Arizona State University, he met some people from Hope Church Movement, and they became his friends. He attended Survivor Weekend, and based on the people and the event, decided to start attending church at Hope. Eventually, he gave his life to Christ and was baptized. I am, quite literally, eternally grateful for what God has done through this church."

Rich Romo
Parent of Student

ACKNOWLEDGMENTS

Art and Nancy Allen – Around 1970, you started a conversation with my parents during one of my swim team practices. That conversation sparked a curiosity to learn more about the gospel and it ultimately led to their conversion 14 weeks later. Thank you for your willingness to live on mission because that decision absolutely changed our family tree. I also made a lifelong friend with your son, Kirk.

My parents, Dr. Clinton (11/30/1929-9/25/2020) and Margaret Smith – Thank you for your unwavering commitment to Jesus, each other, my brothers and me. I love you both.

My brothers, Dan, Marc and Kevin – I couldn't have chosen a better set of brothers than the three of you. Thanks for your brotherhood, epic memories, moments of friction and countless laughs we've shared over the years.

Lance Olson – As a young campus missionary, you were my first financial partner! Thank you for 3 decades of support and encouragement, but most importantly, thank you for your lifelong friendship.

Geoff Zwemke – We were friends in high school and then roommates as freshmen in college, where we had a combined GPA of 2.9. (You had a 2.0 and I had … academic probation!) As I look back over the decades, I'm thankful for all the memories of following Jesus together, ministering to young men together and raising our families together.

My fraternity brother, Ian, and my campus pastor, Steve – Thank you for literally loving the "hell" out of me when I lived in my fraternity and for leading me to Jesus. I'm eternally grateful.

Rob Painter – For almost 40 years, you've been a friend who's stuck closer than a brother. Wendy and I deeply love and appreciate you and Aimee.

Ken Dew – I'm forever grateful to you for starting a conversation with my wife, Wendy, when she was a college student and for leading her to the Lord. You're a gospel hero and it's a privilege to labor together on college campuses.

Gregg Tipton and Britt Woodall – We've had each others' backs through the highs and lows of life and ministry for the past 35 years. Thanks for being brothers and co-laborers in the Kingdom of God.

Al Ells, Gary Kinnaman and Mark Buckley – Your mentorship, wisdom and friendship have shaped our church movement more than you'll ever know. Thank you for being pillars in my life and for literally walking through the fire with Wendy and I.

Jon and Beth Bennett – Thank you for being dear friends to Wendy and I for decades. We've deeply appreciated your support, friendship and investment in our ministry.

The Grace Association, City Pastors, Better Together and Next Level Relational Network – Thank you for being a consistent source of coaching and camaraderie.

My comedian brothers, Bone Hampton, Ron Pearson, Leland Klassen and Thor Ramsey – You're the Outlaw Comedy veterans who believed in our vision to bless students with comedy during their first week on campus! Thank you for always giving it your all when you performed … except for that one time you didn't! Haha.

The original Hope Church Movement team who are still walking alongside us, Corey and Ami, Mike and Jean, Jason and Katie, Ricky, Troy and Rachel, and Rob and Aimee – In 2004, you sold homes, changed jobs, relocated your families and laid your lives down for Arizona State University students. Thank you for going all in.

To everyone who has served on the Hope Church Movement Board of Directors, Corey Vale, Mike McElroy, Dan Saftig, Ray Jensen and Tommy McGeorge – Over the years, you've held my arms up and stood with Wendy and I through the highs and lows of ministry. Thank you for your faithfulness, friendship and faith.

The Hope Church Movement staff – Each of you are on the front lines winning the Battle to Belong on college campuses. Thank you for your commitment to Jesus, our church and the next generation.

My editing team, Ricky, Abraham, Hillary, Matt, Brenna, Mackenzie, Jessie, Leslie, Gary and Joseph – Thank you for helping me compile, clarify and craft the story of what God *has done and is continuing to do*, in and through Hope Church Movement.

The members of Hope Church Movement – In many ways, this book is your story. You've embraced the calling to be a family on mission and I firmly believe that the best is yet to come for us as a movement.

To everyone who isn't mentioned by name but has been a part of our story, thank you!

INTRODUCTION

20

1. THE BATTLE TO BELONG

24

2. THE FISH ARE STILL BITING

52

3. THE STRATEGY

76

4. IMPACT EVENTS: BREAKING THE STIGMA ON COLLEGE CAMPUSES

88

5. AUTHENTIC RELATIONSHIPS: GUIDES WHO COME ALONGSIDE

112

6. ACTION TRUMPS EVERYTHING

134

APPENDIX. LESSONS WE'VE LEARNED OVER THE YEARS

146

INTRO-DUCTION

In the 16th century, the great reformer Martin Luther warned that if we stopped reaching the next generation for Christ, schools would become "the great gates of hell."[1]

It seems that Martin Luther was prophetic.

Secular universities are a breeding ground for new atheism, widespread sexual confusion, anti-biblical rhetoric, and a growing mental health crisis.

As a collegiate-focused church, we've witnessed the state of the next generation firsthand. Since 2004, we've interviewed almost 300,000 college students on more than 50 campuses across America (from San Diego State to Penn State). We've discovered that 96% of college students don't have a biblical understanding of the gospel or how to have a relationship with Jesus.[2] The Barna Group discovered the same thing in their research. A few years ago, they reported that only 4% of Generation Z (the current generation on college campuses) have a biblical worldview.[3]

Does that concern you? It concerns me.

When most Christians think of "unreached people," they

picture mission fields in the developing world or in the 10/40 window. These are legitimate mission fields. But I submit that the most strategic, unreached people group in the world is right in our own backyard: the 20 million college students of America.[4]

So, what's the key to reaching the next generation on college campuses?

Many people think the key is winning the *Battle to Believe,* which is all about helping college students repent and believe in Jesus during this critical time in their lives. Don't get me wrong, I'm all about winning the Battle to Believe on college campuses! We're all called to fulfill the Great Commission and preach the gospel. But this book is not primarily a textbook or guide on how to help students repent and believe in Jesus.

THE BATTLE TO BELONG IS THE UNIVERSAL CRISIS FOR CONNECTION

Before we can win the Battle to Believe, which is the ultimate battle we must win, we have to win the *Battle to Belong.* The Battle to Belong is the universal crisis for connection. It's the internal crisis that students experience when they leave family and friends, arrive on campus for the first time and are desperate for connection. For the longest time, we didn't know what to name this battle. But 10 years ago, we decided to name it the Battle to Belong, and I believe that winning this battle precedes and paves the way to winning the battle of helping students believe in Jesus.

Thankfully, my wife and I were both reached with the gospel as college students at our respective universities. When we were young Christians, we heard church leaders say things like, "If you change the campus, you'll change the world,"[5] and we believed them. That was almost 40 years ago, and we've never left the campus. Instead, we've devoted our lives to winning the Battle to Belong in order to help college students find and follow Jesus, walk in freedom, and live on mission.

I don't consider myself a philosopher, a theologian, or a scholar. I'm a practitioner who has been reaching college students for more than three decades. I was reluctant to write a book for many years, but mentors and leaders in the body of Christ have encouraged me to share what we've learned about the Battle to Belong and the strategy we've developed over the last 20 years.

By the grace of God, we've grown from one church reaching one college campus to a collegiate-focused church-planting movement with multiple sites reaching more than 20 campuses in the southwest. Our leadership team is made up of more than 300 staff, students, and graduates, and more than 85% of them are under the age of 30 years old. Over the last 18 years, we've hosted 48,500 Bible studies and prayed with more than 2,300 people to surrender their lives to Jesus.[6] We're continually blown away by the passion of our church family to live on mission and we're grateful for the story that God is writing in and through our movement.

As my brother-in-law Captain Steven T. Bissell, a retired captain in the United States Marine Corps, once told me, "The Army wins wars, but Marines win battles." If we want to win the war for the next generation, we must win the Battle to Belong on college campuses.

By the time you finish this book, I hope:
- You'll have a new vision for what God wants to do on college campuses.
- You'll be filled with a new passion to connect with college students.
- And you'll be willing to take action and do your part to win the Battle to Belong.

Brian Smith Sr.
Founding and Senior Pastor
Hope Church Movement

If you'd like to stay updated on the latest with Hope Church Movement, scan the QR code below:

01
THE
BATTLE
TO
BELONG

universal crisis for connection

"I came to campus with a list of things I told myself I'd never do. I didn't want to get drunk, have sex, or do drugs. Within three days of being on campus, all those things happened."

– Student at a Pac-12 University

RECRUITMENT CENTERS

College campuses are recruitment centers. Think about it – everyone recruits. Athletics does it. Greek Life does it. Clubs and organizations do it. Even credit card companies do it. They're all trying to recruit students because college students are the future leaders of our nation and the world.

Christians do the same thing. We may call it "evangelism" or "outreach," but at the end of the day, we want to recruit college students to follow Jesus, reach their peers, and leave their campuses better than they found them.

With that in mind, here's a question that has deeply bothered me for years: "Why are so many other organizations better at recruiting college students than the church of the living God?" Don't skip over that question too quickly. Ask yourself again, "Why are so many other organizations better at recruiting college students than the church of the living God?"

That was my experience.

MY FIRST THREE DAYS

Within my first three days of moving onto campus as a college freshman, two students I had never met knocked on my
residence hall door. They knew my name, what high school
I attended, and that I played varsity basketball. They took
time to get to know me and helped me feel welcome during
one of the most important transitions of my life. They were
there to recruit me.

Those two guys were some of the best "evangelists"
I've ever met. But they weren't from a local church; they
were from a social fraternity on campus. The funny thing
is, the last thing my dad told me before I left for college
was, "Son, don't join a fraternity." The first thing I did when
I got to college was… join a fraternity! That day, those two
guys connected with me and invited me to a fraternity party
that weekend, which temporarily soothed my freshman insecurities and instantly helped me feel like I belonged. You
see, underneath my party guy exterior, I was in a crisis. I
was deeply insecure and afraid of being rejected. So, the
first opportunity I had to be a part of something, I took it. I
felt recruited into something bigger than myself. Something
I could belong to.

The internal crisis I experienced during my first three
days at college is the same battle every freshman experiences when they get to campus, especially the first 72
hours. This is the Battle to Belong. Looking back on my
story, I realize that I was in a perfect storm. My freshman
insecurities (rooted in the fear of rejection), mixed with my

desire to sin nature and the lack of intentional recruitment from other Christians, resulted in me getting swept up in the secular campus culture until my junior year. As I walked around campus, I heard open-air preachers and saw Christian clubs tabling, but none of them ever engaged me with the level of intentionality and passion that the two fraternity guys did at my residence hall. Don't get me wrong, I'm not a victim. I'm responsible for the decisions I made. At the same time, I was never personally engaged or recruited by any Christians when I got to campus. I avoided them and it seemed like they avoided me as well.

Within one weekend, my collegiate course was set. I had found my people. Don't miss this. My first three days on campus set my course for the next three years, and that course was in the complete opposite direction of anything having to do with God.

MY FIRST THREE DAYS ON CAMPUS SET MY COURSE FOR THE NEXT THREE YEARS

MY NEXT THREE YEARS

Now here's the thing. In those three years I had a lot of fun, and I accomplished a lot by the world's standards. I played collegiate water polo, I was Interfraternity Council President, and out of the 2,000 fraternity men on my campus, I was selected Greek Man of the Year.

But deep down, I was a mess. In fact, by the spring semester of my freshman year, my decisions had led me to a point where I was willing to admit that I was in a crisis. I felt lost, isolated, confused and I even considered dropping out of college. The bad decisions continued until my junior year, when God intersected my life in a profound way. (I'll share more about that story later.)

I REMEMBER

One of the main reasons I've devoted my life to reaching college students with the gospel is because *I remember* what it was like when I first got to campus. *I remember* the insecurities. *I remember* the peer pressure. *I remember* the intense desire to belong. *I also remember* the three years that I wasted. At the time of writing, the upcoming 2023 fall semester will be exactly 40 years since my freshman year. I can honestly say, I'm more passionate than ever about reaching college students, and it's simply because "*I remember.*"

All throughout scripture, we see the importance and power of remembering. In Deuteronomy 8, Moses charged the people of God to remember where they came from. In Psalm 143:5, it says, "I remember the days of old…"

A STUDENT'S PERSPECTIVE

"I remember my dad had just left and I'd finished unpacking. I was sitting in my room by myself, watching Netflix on my laptop. And I started to tear up because I just felt so alone. All I remember thinking was, 'This can't be it. This can't be it to my college life.' My dad had told me, 'Don't forget what we taught you, don't lose yourself.' And within the first day, I felt like I was losing myself."

    – 18-year-old male student from Philadelphia, PA

WE MUST REMEMBER

FORGOTTEN FRESHMEN

The unfortunate reality is that almost everybody forgets what it's like to be a new freshman. We tend to remember the high points of our college years: the football games, the friends we made and, especially, graduation. But most people forget about the inner turmoil they felt the first 72 hours they got to campus. As that time in our lives becomes a distant memory, we overlook the insecurities we had as freshmen and brush off the desperation we felt to belong in a new foreign environment. That's why I call them *Forgotten Freshmen*. When we lose touch with the internal crisis that freshmen face and what they truly need, we lose the ability to reach them effectively. We must remember.

That's why our leadership team takes time before the start of every school year to remind ourselves of what it was like when we first arrived on campus. Recalling our own personal experiences gives us fresh vision, passion, and empathy for the incoming freshman class. It reminds us of the reality of what students face, and it compels us to lay down our lives to reach the next generation. Do you remember what it was like for you?

A STUDENT'S PERSPECTIVE

"College felt like an opportunity to reinvent myself. Like if I hid all the ugly parts of my life and my insecurities then I'd be accepted. Freshman year honestly felt really dark, like I was doing it on my own."

— 19-year-old female student from Oakley, CA

WHAT IS THE BATTLE TO BELONG?

Every fall semester, millions of students around America step foot on their college campuses for the first time. It's their first time living on their own and everything is new. They have new roommates, new classes, and, of course, new mini fridges. Most are living in a new city, many in a new state or even a new country. Imagine jumping into a swift current with no boat, no gear, and no guide. That's what the first 72 hours on campus feels like for many freshmen.

Internally, there's a mix of excitement and anxiety, hopes and fears, dreams and doubts. They're anxious to connect and form friendships, because belonging is a fundamental

OUR NEED TO BELONG IS A GOD-GIVEN DESIRE

need for every human being. Psychologists agree that all of us are searching for closeness, acceptance, a sense of community, and a conviction that we matter as individuals.[1] Our need to belong is a God-given desire. Unfortunately, it's common for many students to be surrounded by thousands of peers yet feel extremely lonely and relationally disconnected.

The Battle to Belong is the internal crisis that students experience when they leave family and friends, arrive on campus for the first time and are desperate for connection. Dr. Steve Shadrach, a campus ministry hero of mine, says it this way: "The students around you are secretly desperate for someone to love them unconditionally and to believe in them."[2]

STUDENT EXPERIENCES

"I would look at my friends' Snapchat and Instagram stories, and see that everyone was having a lot more fun than I was. I'd just compare my college life to theirs. I wasn't expecting to give up on my social life that easily, but I just realized that

finding friends in college was a lot harder than I thought it would be."

— 19-year-old female student from Tempe, AZ

"My parents helped me move into my residence hall and get everything in place. When they left, that's when loneliness really set in. I realized, 'Wow, I'm alone here.' I sat in my room and played video games and I went to the dining hall by myself. I was surrounded by a ton of people, but I spent a lot of my first semester feeling alone."

— 18-year-old male student from Gilbert, AZ

THE RAPID RIVER OF SECULAR CAMPUS CULTURE

Just as the Colorado River carved the Grand Canyon, so campus life has been carved and imprinted by the *Rapid River of Secular Campus Culture.*

College students may not be able to describe it with words, but every one of them has felt the pull of this Rapid River. The Bible describes this current as going with the flow of "the world" - and it's headed in the opposite direction of anything godly.

1 John 2:15-16 says, "Do not love the world nor the things in the world. If anyone loves the world, the love of the Father is not in him. For all that is in the world, the lust of the flesh and the lust of the eyes and the boastful pride of life, is not from the Father, but is from the world."

Ephesians 2:1-3 says, "You were dead in your trespasses and sins, in which you formerly walked according to the course of this world, according to the prince of the power of the air, of the spirit that is now working in the sons of disobedience. Among them we too all formerly lived in the lusts of our flesh, indulging the desires of the flesh and of the mind, and were by nature children of wrath, even as the rest."

In Acts 2:40 NLT, it says Peter was, "Strongly urging all his listeners, 'Save yourselves from this crooked generation.'"

What does the pull of the world look like on college campuses? The current is made up of the unspoken expectation and common knowledge of how to do college life, and it's captured in the simple phrase, *"This is how we do!"* Campus culture screams at every college student, "This is how we do friendships. This is how we do weekends. This is how we do parties. This is how we do classes. This is how we do romance. This is how we do college!"

CAMPUS CULTURE SCREAMS AT EVERY COLLEGE STUDENT – THIS IS HOW WE DO!

None of us had an opportunity to vote on this culture, because it already existed when we got to campus. It's reinforced by students' collective insecurities and their deepest desires for belonging. It promotes spending their collegiate career focused on sin, self, and life lived on their own terms. Campus culture makes sin look fun, but indulging in sin never leads to peace, joy, or fulfillment. Biblically speaking, we know that sin always takes us further than we want to go, costs us more than we want to pay, and keeps us longer than we want to stay.

CAMPUS CULUTRE MAKES SIN LOOK FUN

A STUDENT'S PERSPECTIVE

"I grew up in the church and went to a Christian high school, so going to college my values were pretty set. I wasn't ashamed to say that I was waiting to have sex until marriage. When the guys who lived in my residence hall heard this, some of them made bets with one another about which one of them would get me to lose my virginity."

— 18-year-old female student from Golden, CO

PORN IN A FILM CLASS

Years ago, a freshman student was in his first semester as a film production major, and he experienced the craziness of secular campus culture firsthand. But there wasn't just pressure to "go with the flow" from other students. It was from the professors themselves. He told me he couldn't name a single professor who wasn't using their class to push an ulterior agenda, and those agendas were often anti-biblical.

One of the most poignant examples was a film history class he took with 200 other students. The professor would often talk about his own sexuality, show films with crude scenes, and start discussions about the benefits of watching pornography and masturbation. He encouraged the class that college is a time for everyone should experiment with their sexuality and find out "what floats their boat." He'd also hold in-class debates on political topics and belittle students who disagreed with him. And because this professor was close to being tenured, it was pointless to complain to the administration.

Listen to how this student describes his freshman experience: "Everybody makes college seem like a safe space to speak your mind. Or if you have a different opinion, that's fine because people will respect that. But the way these professors structured their classes was either you agree with them and everyone's happy, or they make you look like a fool for having a different opinion."

THE RED ZONE

The president of a Pac-12 university shared something in a religious council meeting that resonated with my own experience. He said, "The first weekend of a college freshman's experience is a powerful, powerful time. Students are making decisions for the first time away from their parents, and making important, impactful decisions in a very rapid succession. This first weekend is either problematic or opportunistic."

The beginning of the school year is a critical window where students make pivotal decisions about how they're going to navigate college. Unfortunately, negative choices are all too common. In fact, social scientists and universities call the first six weeks of college the *Red Zone* because of the heightened possibility of students making poor decisions, specifically as it relates to sexual assault. In fact, 50% of college sexual assaults happen in the Red Zone[3] and 90% involve alcohol.[4]

I've heard from some university officials that 80% of code of conduct violations are committed by freshmen, and most happen during this time frame when students are being "recruited" in a lot of different directions.

THE BATTLE BEGINS

Make no mistake about it, there's a war over the hearts and minds of college students in our nation, and the battle starts during the first 72 hours students arrive on campus.

Read these students' reflections of what it was like entering the Battle to Belong.

"When you're going to a college party, I think it's pretty common to want to get as drunk as you can so that you fit in with the crowd. I mean, that's definitely what I was trying to do. I

remember I didn't like the way I was acting and thinking to myself, why am I doing this? But then I'd think about how, if I stopped partying, then it would be a really lonely year and really hard to make friends."

— 19-year-old female student from New Berlin, WI

"Those parties were bigger than I thought, just packed with people, and full of drugs, alcohol and vaping. I remember my whole first week was spent partying at this apartment. And I remember thinking, wow, that was fast, I've already found my people. Cool, I'm set."

— 19-year-old female student from Thornton, CO

"I remember thinking to myself that instead of college being the four best years of my life, it was going to be the four loneliest years of my life. I wanted to make friends so badly I started to compromise. I hated who I was becoming."

— 18-year-old female student from Yuma, AZ

A GROWING MENTAL HEALTH CRISIS

Over the years, I've prayed for hundreds of college students who've felt lost, depressed, and even suicidal. These mental health issues are widespread on university campuses. In fact, a recent study discovered that a "lower sense of belonging is significantly associated with greater severity of depression, hopelessness and suicidal ideation."[5] A university official once told me that the two most prescribed medications on their campus at the time were birth control pills and antidepressants. In a 2021 study, 22% of college students screened positive for major depression and 41% screened positive for depression overall. One in three students screened positive for an anxiety disorder.[6]

Just as our church sees the critical importance of helping students belong, it seems the research community is coming to the same conclusion. The revolutionary *Belonging Project* at Stanford University shows that a sense of belonging protects emotional health and personal wellbeing, and helps individuals flourish in all aspects of their lives, even in the midst of adversity and trauma.[7]

THE LONGING FOR BELONGING

Since the beginning of time, mankind has had a deep, God-given need to belong. Every one of us has a longing for belonging. That's why in Genesis 2:18, even before sin entered the world, God told Adam that "it's not good for man to be alone." No member of the Trinity was ever alone – and since Adam was made in God's image, it wasn't good for man to be alone either. Adam wasn't lonely because there was something wrong with him. Adam was lonely because he was made in the image of God and he was never designed to be alone.

A ROUGH PATH

I heard the story of a freshman who came to college and was excited to make new friends and play on the university women's soccer team. However, it was challenging for her to learn how to balance the demands of school and collegiate sports. She also had fears about not fitting in or playing well.

By the end of the fall semester, she stopped looking for a church altogether. "I ended up wandering further and further away from Jesus," she said. "Living for myself led me down a rough path. I struggled with depression and anxiety. It was really painful." Eventually a teammate invited her to a campus church, and she got connected. "God delivered me from depression and anxiety, and now I know true joy and peace in knowing Him. All I want is to know Him and to make Him known," she said. "The fellowship of other believers has built up my faith so much. I get to process what God is doing in my life, develop deep friendships, be held accountable, and I get to learn how to share my story and the gospel."

A STUDENT'S PERSPECTIVE

"It was easy to find drinking, smoking, drugs, and sex in the residence hall even if I wasn't looking for it, but unfortunately I was. I thought because I worked full time and went to school full time without failing any classes, that I was doing okay. But even though I never stopped believing in Jesus, I was still backslidden and wasn't pursuing a relationship with Him.

By freshman year, I was smoking weed and drinking and hooking up with girls. By sophomore year, I lived in an apartment and started selling weed because it made sense somehow as a finance major. By junior year, I was selling a lot more weed and throwing parties to pay the bills and be the 'cool guy' the culture glorified. That's when things started to get out of control and I started to deal with serious anxiety and guilt.

One night after waking up from a dream of a storm coming in my life, I prayed and asked God to help me get out of my lifestyle and redeem me. That day was Good Friday and I didn't even realize it.

Later that night when leaving the library, I heard music on campus and went to go check it out. It was a worship night, and as I stood on the edges of the crowd, a member from Hope Church came up and introduced himself to me and simply started a conversation. He was genuine and asked questions about me. I could tell he actually wanted to know me and cared about me even though we had just met. It was the encouragement I needed to open up about my situation and lifestyle.

Over the next few weeks, my life started to change as I started following Jesus again. I ended some unhealthy relationships and moved out of my old house. Ten days after I moved out, my old roommate got shot five times in a bad drug deal and narrowly escaped death. If God hadn't gotten ahold of me when He did, I would've been there...and I probably wouldn't be here today."

– 19-year-old male student from Portland, OR

WHAT IS THE REAL WORLD?

How many times have you heard someone say to a new college grad, "Congratulations, now you've entered the real world!" While I understand the reason for saying that, I couldn't disagree more. Sadly, I've done far too many memorial services for students. College is real life, and college students make real decisions, with real consequences in this life and for eternity.

- College isn't just "practice for real life."
- It isn't just a time to "sow your wild oats."
- And it isn't "God's blind spot."
- College is the real world – and the Battle to Belong has real consequences.

COLLEGE STUDENTS MAKE REAL DECISIONS, WITH REAL CONSEQUENCES

THE BATTLE TO BELIEVE

Unfortunately many Christians *aren't aware of the Battle to Belong*, but they *are aware of the Battle to Believe.* In other words, they understand the importance of helping college students believe in Jesus during this critical time in their lives. After all, studies have shown that 97% of people who become Christians do so before the age of 30 years old.[8] That's a mind-blowing statistic – out of every 100 Christians only three surrendered their lives to Jesus after turning 30. Reaching college students for Jesus is perhaps the most strategic investment a ministry can make.

We desperately need to help students understand the Bible, believe the gospel and follow Jesus as Lord.

As a church movement, we're passionate about equipping every church member to clarify the gospel. In fact, 60% of our members were won to the Lord through our ministry. Every month, we host more than 800 evangelistic Bible studies on college campuses and their surrounding cities. The gospel is clarified during every Sunday service because 50% of the attendees are visitors and the majority are unchurched or unfamiliar with Christianity. Then, after service, our leadership team leads Gospel Appointments with these visitors over lunch.

GOSPEL APPOINTMENTS

A *Gospel Appointment* is simply a time to clarify the gospel with someone. It's when we take the time to listen to someone's story and then tell our story and the gospel story. These appointments are extremely effective because they're personal, relational, and intentional. Over the last three years, we've shared the gospel with 9,300 people and many students have chosen to follow Jesus with their lives.[9]

I'm so thankful for Paul and David Worcester's training on Gospel Appointments.[10] Their training has revolutionized our ministry and multiplied our effectiveness. Our whole leadership team is trained on how to clarify the gospel by using a conversational tool called *The Gospel Story.* You can use the QR code below to access it.

JESUS WON THE BATTLE TO BELONG AND THE BATTLE TO BELIEVE

When we look closely at the ministry of Jesus, we discover that He won the Battle to Belong with His disciples before He won the Battle to Believe. Throughout the Gospels, Jesus called His disciples to do three things: Come and See, Come and Die, and Go and Tell (Matthew 28:16-20).
I submit:

- Come and See is about winning the Battle to Belong (John 1:33-35).
- Come and Die is about winning the Battle to Believe (Matthew 16:24-26).
- Go and Tell is about winning the Battle to Become Fishers of Men (Mark 1:17).

Jesus' ultimate goal was to send His disciples out to preach the gospel and win the world. But before He invited them to "come and die" or "go and tell," He invited them to "come and see." Some biblical timelines even suggest that it was over two years from when Jesus first invited His disciples to "come and see" to when Jesus revealed Himself as the Christ and invited His disciples to "come and die" in Matthew 16.

When the disciples first asked Jesus where He was staying, He simply said, "Come and see" (John 1:39 NLT). Can you imagine Jesus, God in human flesh, inviting you to hang out? Seems like a good approach, considering most scholars believe the disciples were between the ages of 15-20 (the age of most high school and college students today). Jesus didn't invite them to talk about some deep theology, He welcomed them into His life to have a real relationship with Him. In other words, He invited them to belong even before they believed.

WHICH COMES FIRST: BELONGING OR BELIEVING?

Remember the ancient riddle, "Which came first, the chicken or the egg?" Consider this: "Which comes first, belonging or believing?" There are plenty of times where people repent and believe in Jesus without belonging to a Christian community. From time to time, our campus missionaries have divine appointments with students who are ready to surrender their lives to Jesus the first time they hear the gospel. There are also gifted evangelists, like my friend Dr. Rice Broocks, who leads events like *God's Not Dead* on college campuses across the country.[11] At his events, he presents compelling scientific and scriptural evidence for Christianity and many students make the decision to repent and believe in Jesus.

Can students believe in Jesus before they belong to a Christian community? Absolutely – but in my experience it's not the norm.

EVERYBODY IS OPEN TO FRIENDSHIP

The reality is that the majority of students we meet on campus are not immediately open to the gospel (that was the case in my story). They may be open to exploring their faith, but they're not yet ready to go all in and follow Jesus.

On the other hand, we've discovered that almost every college student is looking for two things, whether they're aware of it or not: they want to *have fun and make friends fast.*

As a young evangelist, my pastor used to say, "Everybody's open to the gospel someday, and somebody's open today." When it comes to friendship, I like to say, "Everybody is open to friendship someday, and a ton of people are open to it today."

Just like Jesus started with "Come and See," we start by inviting students to come hang out with us. In fact, at any given point, our ministry is in relationship with more than 3,500 students from 20 college campuses.[12] Not all of them are actively attending church or a Bible study, but we continue to invest in the relationships and try to love them the way Jesus would. When they inevitably hit a crisis, we want them to know that we're here for them.

CRISIS TRIANGLE

Isn't it true that many of us who became Christians did so after a crisis in our lives? That was the case for me. In fact, sometimes the "kindness of God" that leads us to repentance takes the form of a crisis in our lives.

Years ago, two mentors in my life, Rev. Alfred Ells and Dr. Gary Kinnaman, introduced me to *The Crisis Triangle*.[13] This has become a paradigm-shaping principle for our ministry. Here's how it works:

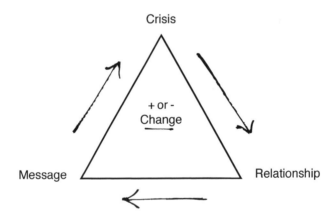

Whenever someone hits a crisis, the people they have a relationship with will determine the message they hear –

either the message of the gospel, or the message of secular campus culture. And the message they hear leads to either positive or negative change in their lives. Every college student hits crisis. Some are willing to admit it right away but for some it takes longer. That's why our rally cry every year is to "meet a ton of people and make a bunch of friends." We want to be in relationship with as many students as possible so that when they hit crisis, we can bring the gospel message into their lives.

EVERY COLLEGE STUDENT HITS CRISIS

TWO WEEKENDS IN A HOSPITAL

A few years ago, a freshman student connected with a member from our church who was passing out water bottles and welcoming students to campus. They hung out a few times, but then lost touch once the freshman started hanging out with a different group of friends involved in the party scene. During his experience in the Battle to Belong, he was recruited and swept up in the Rapid River of Secular Campus Culture.

Later in the year, that student ended up in the hospital two weekends in a row with alcohol poisoning. Both times he woke up in the hospital and none of his "friends" from the night before were there. The only thing he remembered was the doctor saying, "Young man, your friends don't care about you." He was in a crisis. His decisions during his first few weeks on campus almost led to him losing his life a few months later. Thankfully, during his moment of crisis at the hospital, that student remembered the guy from Hope Church he'd met on campus at the beginning of the year. A couple of days after he left the hospital, he reached out to that member for help, joined a Bible study, and soon after surrendered his life to Jesus.

THE BATTLE TO BELONG PRECEDES THE BATTLE TO BELIEVE

Before we can win the Battle to Believe, which is the ulti-mate battle we must win, we must win the Battle to Belong. Some call it pre-evangelism and some call it earning the right to be heard. Regardless of what we call it, I believe it's the key ingredient for reaching college students. Often, winning this battle precedes and paves the way for helping students believe the gospel.

In my experience, most students aren't coming up to me asking, "What must I do to be saved?" It happens, but it's rare. If we're serious about reaching the next generation of college students, we need a strategy to help students feel like they belong to Christian community - *even before they believe.* Keep in mind that when I say "belong to a Christian community," I'm not talking about formal membership, I'm talking about students experiencing meaningful friendship with other Christians before they're saved.

NATURAL BIRTH AND SPIRITUAL BIRTH

In John 3, Jesus equated salvation with being "born again." We know that Jesus was talking about a spiritual truth but consider a natural birth for a moment. Before babies are born into the world, they have a place to belong: their mothers womb. In the womb they are protected, receive nutrients, oxygen, and everything else they need to develop until they're ready to be born.

Do you see where this is headed? As people are counting the costs of following Jesus, what if they had a Christian community to belong to as they grow in their understanding of God before they're born again?

Dr. Carlton Fong, a researcher studying the importance of belonging at Texas State University, told me that when people feel like they belong it unlocks something in them. It unlocks new motivation, new engagement, new persistence, new openness, new curiosity, and a willingness to try something new. What does that suggest for us?

It tells us that when the people of God help students feel like they belong, it unlocks within students an openness to the gospel and a willingness to try something new: namely, to welcome Christian friendship and eventually trust Jesus with their lives.

WE CAN HELP PEOPLE BELONG BEFORE THEY BELIEVE

In other words, we can help people *belong before they believe*. Winning the Battle to Belong isn't just a good idea; it's a life and death rescue mission. It's impossible to exaggerate the urgency of this mission because students' lives are literally hanging in the balance.

But to see victory, we've got to stop playing defense and start playing offense.

CHAPTER SUMMARY

Reaching college students for Jesus is the most strategic investment a ministry can make. But if we're going to be successful, we must engage in the Battle to Belong. The Battle to Belong is the internal crisis that students experience when they leave family and friends, arrive on campus for the first time and are desperate for connection. Winning this battle often precedes and paves the way for us to win the Battle to Believe.

QUESTIONS TO CONSIDER

1. Do you remember what it was like to be a college freshman? What were your first three days on campus like? What were you hopeful about? Anxious about? Insecure about?

2. How have you experienced the power of belonging in your own life?

3. In your ministry context, what could it look like to help people belong before they believe?

02
THE
FISH
ARE *still*
BITING

"The best offense… is a good offense."

GREEKS ARE GREAT EVANGELISTS

I'm proud to be a member of Phi Delta Theta fraternity. I've developed lifelong friendships with other Phi Delts and I still serve as a faculty member. Every year, my fraternity brothers and I were determined to recruit (or "rush", like we called it in the 80s) from the incoming freshman class and that's exactly what we did. In fact, we quadrupled the size of our chapter over the course of four years. In nearly 175 years of its existence, Phi Delta Theta has expanded to 290 campuses and initiated more than 278,000 men. It currently has 193 chapters and approximately 178,000 living alumni.[1] I think it's safe to say that the recruitment strategy for Phi Delt, and many other fraternities, is working.

On the other hand, research shows that the median age of an American church is only 73 years old.[2] That tells us that half of the churches in America have only been around for about one generation. I believe Christians can learn something about recruiting and multiplying from the Greek system. Every fall semester, Greek organizations employ an urgent and relational recruitment strategy because they understand that there's a limited window of time to connect with incoming freshmen. If they're not successful, they won't survive as an organization.

How much more critical is it that we connect with every freshman class for the kingdom of God? Campus ministries need to be urgent and relational in their strategy to reach the incoming freshman class. If we don't, we'll lose the next generation and our ministries ultimately won't survive. It's like my friend Paul Worcester says, "Give me freshmen or give me death."[3]

THE FIRST RECRUITER

Have you ever thought of God as a recruiter?

After Adam and Eve sinned in Genesis 3, they didn't immediately experience physical death, but they did die spiritually. Sin entered the world and their connection with God was broken. However, that didn't stop God – He came looking. Just like God the Father went looking for Adam and Eve, Jesus said in Luke 19:10 that He came to "seek and to save that which was lost." To seek is to recruit. Jesus is building His church, and He's recruiting sons and daughters to join His team. I believe there's a part of everyone of us that wants to be recruited. We want others to see the potential within us and be recruited to join something bigger than ourselves.

God is a recruiter. He didn't wait for Adam and Eve to come to Him; He went to them. Jesus didn't wait for lost people to come to Him and discover that He was the Messiah. Jesus came to seek and save that which was lost.

In the same way, we can't wait for lost people to come to us – we have to go to them. Like I said earlier, we can call it "evangelism" or "outreach"; whatever we call it, if we boil it down to its essence… it's recruiting.

WE'VE GOTTA GO TO THEM

It's common for ministries to play it safe and wait for people to come to them. They don't believe what Jesus said, that "the harvest is plentiful," so they don't believe students are open to the gospel. Many have a scarcity mindset. They allow themselves to be intimidated by the secular culture on campus. They feel like they can't compete with college parties.

Here's what it looks like to play it safe:
- Hanging up fliers around campus… instead of personally engaging students on campus.
- Standing behind promotional tables… but not starting conversations with students as they walk by.
- Putting on events that lack creativity and mostly attract students with Christian backgrounds… instead of unreached and unchurched students.
- Hosting a college service once a week and waiting for students to show up… instead of going on campus and bringing them to service with you.
- Campus ministry leaders trying to do all of the planning, setup and ministry themselves… instead of equipping student leaders to connect with, pray for, and share their stories with their peers.
- Shrinking back from sharing the gospel because of negative responses from students or organizations on campus.

That's not the vision Jesus had for His followers. Scripture is clear that Jesus and the original disciples envisioned a church that was always advancing, no matter the opposition, persecution, or cultural expectations. If we're going to win the Battle to Belong and reach college students, we need to change how we think about the church *and* about the lost.

THREE TRUTHS WE NEED TO EMBRACE

1. The church should be on the offensive.

To clarify, we shouldn't *intentionally be offensive*. We should intentionally be *on* the offensive. There's a big difference!

The first time Jesus used the word "church" in the New Testament, He used it in the context of war.

"I also say to you that you are Peter, and upon this rock I will build My church; and the gates of Hades will not overpower it. I will give you the keys of the kingdom of heaven; and whatever you bind on earth shall have been bound in heaven, and whatever you loose on earth shall have been loosed in heaven." Matthew 16:18-19

Gates are designed to defend. They're stationary – they don't move forward or take new territory. They're supposed to keep some people in and others out. When Jesus says the gates of hell won't overpower the church, it signifies that the kingdom of hell is on the defensive and the local church is on the offensive. In other words, the church has the power and authority to tear apart the gates of hell. As Pastor J.D. Greear says, "The early church had no building, no money, and no political influence. And they turned the world upside-down."[4]

THE CHURCH HAS THE POWER AND AUTHORITY TO TEAR APART THE GATES OF HELL

The enemy wants us to be intimidated and believe that the church is on the defensive. But that's not the case. Church was never intended to be a "holy huddle" where we attract students who grew up in Christian homes looking to shelter themselves from the college culture. Church was never intended to be about "trading baseball cards" and simply recruiting Christians from other churches into ours. Sadly, this is more common than you might think. According to Ed Stetzer and Mike Breen, 96% of church growth is transfer growth.[5]

The church is an invasive, gate-taking force intended to break into the enemy's strongholds and rescue the lost.

It's a battleship perfectly designed to accomplish a noble mission, not a cruise ship catered to the comforts of its passengers.

USS MIDWAY

A few years ago in San Diego, my family and I toured the USS Midway, a retired aircraft carrier.

The Midway has a rich history. It was built near the end of World War II and was the largest ship in the world for the next 10 years. It was used throughout the Vietnam War, the Cold War and in Operation Desert Storm. I think it's safe to say this ship helped change the destiny of our nation.

While on the tour, I noticed how everything was created with a purpose, from the length of the deck (perfectly designed for planes to take off of), to the engine room, to the mess hall, to the crew quarters. As I visited these different rooms, I began to feel a sense of awe. Then it hit me: I was a civilian on a battleship! That ship wasn't built for comfort, convenience, or happiness. It was built for war.

That's a picture of the local church. The church is like a battleship designed and fitted for war, with a crew that's focused on a mission.

CRUISE SHIP OR BATTLESHIP

There are two competing ways to view the church. Cruise ships are entertaining, comfortable and designed to meet our every need. Battleships are outfitted for battle, instead of comfort, and designed to accomplish a mission. To be completely candid, a part of me really wants the church to be more like a cruise ship. Especially in my late 50s, a cruise sounds incredible – unlimited food, amateur karaoke, comedy shows, and strolls on the lido deck. Unfortunately, many people have strayed from God's original design for the church.

The church is a group of people who are following one Master (Jesus), preaching one message (the gospel) and living out one mission (to reach the lost). It's not just a place we go to hear a message. The church is a group of people, with a message, on the move. We should be on the offensive, advancing the gospel of Jesus on our campuses and surrounding cities.

THE CHURCH IS A GROUP OF PEOPLE, WITH A MESSAGE, ON THE MOVE

I like to say that Hope Church Movement is a *family on mission*. We're not one *or* the other. We're both. Let me explain.

A church that's "all family but no mission" is a lot like a hippie commune – comfortable and complacent with a lot of sitting around. Pastor J.D. Greear said it well: "Without a mission, a church is not a church. It's just a group of dis-obedient Christians hanging out."[6] We aren't supposed to wait around until we go to heaven. Jesus sends us into the world to *win the world*. At the same time, a church that's "all mission and no family" is like a bunch of robots who do activities together but lack any real relationship. We aren't just a *family* and we're not just on a *mission*. We're a family on mission called to win the Battle to Belong and fulfill the Great Commission on college campuses.

2. We're all called to become fishers of men.

In Mark 1:14-18, Jesus gave us a vision of what the Christian life should be like. It's become one of my life verses.

Now after John had been taken into custody, Jesus came into Galilee, preaching the gospel of God, and saying, "The time is fulfilled, and the kingdom of God is at hand; repent and believe in the gospel." As He was going along by the Sea of Galilee, He saw Simon and Andrew, the brother of Simon, casting a net in the sea; for they were fishermen. And Jesus said to them, "Follow Me, and I will make you become fishers of men." Immediately they left their nets and followed Him.

This passage isn't only for full-time ministers, but for ev-eryone following Jesus. We're all called to repent and follow Jesus, and then He'll make us become fishers of men. A question I often ask our church members is, "If you aren't

becoming a fisher of men, are you really following Jesus?"
The call to become a "fisher of men" is included in the call to
follow Jesus. It's a package deal. Missionary Hudson Taylor
once said, "The Great Commission is not an option to be
considered; it is a command to be obeyed."[7]

Consider these statistics:
- 95% of all Christians have never led anyone to
  Christ.[8]
- Only 2% of Christians will invite an unchurched person to their church in a year.[9]
- 47% of Millennial Christians believe that it's wrong
  to share one's personal beliefs with someone of a
  different faith in hopes that they will one day share
  that faith.[10]

PERSONAL, NOT PRIVATE

Although our relationship with Jesus is personal, it was never designed to be private. Imagine if I was ashamed to tell
people that Wendy was my wife, and my excuse was, "It's
a private relationship. It's just me and Wendy. And I don't
want to offend anybody and make them feel uncomfortable
because she's such an amazing wife." Not only is that ridic-
ulous, it's offensive to my wife!

That's regrettably what many people do with Jesus.
They're ashamed to talk about their relationship with Christ,
so they edit Him out of their lives and they miss out on becoming fishers of men.

KEEPERS OF THE AQUARIUM

Years ago, Paul Harvey said, "We've strayed from being fishers of men, to being keepers of the aquarium."[11] It's easy to get comfortable taking care of the Christians in our congregation while reaching the unreached takes a backseat. We won't rub shoulders with any unreached students if we stay inside our church building, but we'll cross paths with thousands of lost souls if we walk around campus. Jesus was all about reaching the lost, so that's what we should do, too.

Remember in Luke 7:34, the Pharisees accused Jesus of being a friend of sinners (I think it would be awesome to be accused of that!). The important thing is that even though Jesus was a friend of sinners, Jesus never sinned. We should be willing to build relationships and reach students by all means possible, short of sinning ourselves.

That's how the Apostle Paul lived. I think we can all agree that Paul didn't play "not to lose"; he played to win!

Listen to how Paul describes his evangelistic mindset in 1 Corinthians 9:19-25:

For though I am free from all men, I have made myself a slave to all, so that I may win more. To the Jews I became as a Jew, so that I might win Jews; to those who are under the Law, as under the Law though not being myself under the Law, so that I might win those who are under the Law; to those who are without law, as without law, though not being without the law of God but under the law of Christ, so that I might win those who are without law. To the weak I became weak, that I might win the weak; I have become all things to all men, so that I may by all means save some. I do all things for the sake of the gospel, so that I may become a fellow partaker of it. Do you not know that those who run in a race all run, but only one receives the prize? Run in such a way that you may win. Everyone who competes in the games exercises self-control in all things. They then do it to receive a perishable wreath, but we an imperishable.

Paul's life revolved around doing whatever it took to reach the lost. In Romans 15:20 NLT, he said, "My ambition has always been to preach the Good News where the name of Christ has never been heard."

His goal wasn't to be a "keeper of the aquarium." Paul was laser-focused on becoming a fisher of men. Think about it. In Matthew 28, when Jesus said to "go and make disciples," He didn't say to go find Christians (because there weren't any). He said to go find sinners, win them into the kingdom, and make disciples out of them. Jesus said, "Go". The Great Commission was never about waiting for people to come to the church; it's always been about the church going to them.

For all of us following Jesus, we're called to make the Great Commission our mission, regardless of our degree or vocation. We're called to be a witness for Jesus, regardless of our spiritual gifts, age, stage of life, or current circumstances. Our church is intentional about keeping the main thing, the main thing. Everything we do revolves around evangelism, and as members of our church have embraced this truth, there have been incredible testimonies.

WE'RE ALL CALLED TO MAKE THE GREAT COMMISSION OUR MISSION

BLEACHER MINISTRY

My wife Wendy has lived this out in a profound way over the years. When our sons were in junior high and high school, she had, what I informally called, her "Bleacher Ministry."

While at our sons' sporting events, she would walk across the bleachers and start conversations with different people in the crowd. She would introduce herself, get to know them, and build friendships with them over the course of the season. Some people got saved and others got reconnected to churches because of those conversations. All because she was willing to walk across the bleacher.

BOOT CAMP REVIVAL

There's a member of our church who surrendered his life to Jesus as a college student, learned about the Great Commission, and started reaching out to his family and friends.

He was passionate about reaching the lost. Several years later, he joined the army. While in Basic Combat Training for three months, he sensed God giving him an opportunity to reach his fellow soldiers.

Here's what he did: He offered to pray for soldiers who were stressed about their future or had become injured during training. If they gave him permission, he'd even pray for them on the spot and record it in a journal so he could follow up and ask how things were going. He also wrote letters home to his wife with specific prayer requests, so she could be praying as well. During those three months, many soldiers experienced God healing them or their family members.

Something amazing happened one night while they were asleep in their bunks. They heard a soldier start crying uncontrollably. He had just read a letter from home saying that his mom had a terminal brain cancer diagnosis. Our church member gathered a handful of other soldiers, and they started praying for God to heal his mom. The next day, that soldier received some miraculous news. When he called his mom, she had just been told by the doctors that the brain cancer had disappeared overnight – the very same night they had prayed! As you can imagine, that deeply impacted every soldier who heard the news.

This and other stories sent shockwaves throughout the whole training company of 164 soldiers. What began as just a handful of soldiers following Jesus eventually turned into 95 soldiers marching to church on Sundays. Many repented and were even baptized while at Basic Combat Training, all because one soldier decided to live with an eternal perspective, take the Great Commission seriously, and be a fisher of men.

A PERSONAL TRAINER ON MISSION

Another member of our church learned to share his testimony and the gospel as a college student. After graduation, he started working as a strength and conditioning coach for young athletes, and he sensed God calling him to become a fisher of men at his job. The men in his Connect Group encouraged him to ask God to use him to reach those around him.

He started praying before training sessions and looking for opportunities to encourage his clients. At the end of a session, he offered to pray for them. As he stepped out in faith, he began to see God opening doors. Some clients became friends and he was able to share his faith with them.

One week, God put it on his heart to begin hosting a Bible study to help the athletes understand the gospel. They started going through our church's *Red Book*, which is a Bible study explaining the basics of Christianity. At first it was only a few guys, but as they continued, more people attended. By the end of the semester there were 25 people attending the Bible study. Five of those young men surrendered their lives to Jesus and two were baptized!

No matter our vocation, we're all called to become fishers of men.

3. The harvest is plentiful on college campuses.

Matthew 9 records an incredible promise from Jesus:

Jesus was going through all the cities and villages, teaching in their synagogues and proclaiming the gospel of the kingdom, and healing every kind of disease and every kind of sickness. Seeing the people, He felt compassion for them, because they were distressed and dispirited like sheep without a shepherd. Then He said to His disciples, "The harvest is plentiful, but the workers are few. Therefore beseech the Lord of the harvest to send out workers into His harvest." Matthew 9:35-38

Jesus looked at the people who were lost, hurting, and broken, and said to His disciples, "The harvest is plentiful." So, for all the campus missionaries out there, that's what I like to call job security! Until there's a new heaven and a new earth, there will always be lost people to reach, and there will always be a need for more workers in the harvest. If you wake up every day and remind yourself of this promise, you'll approach everyone you meet with a new level of intentionality, focus and compassion.

One member in our church had never shared the gospel with anyone because she was afraid nobody wanted to hear the message and they'd reject her. That all changed on one of our Spring Break mission trips. She was talking to a girl at a hangout and set up a Gospel Appointment with her. Later that night, she led her new friend to the Lord. Seeing a peer on campus respond to the gospel, sparked a fire in her to share her story with as many people as she could. The next year, she decided to live on campus as a Resident Assistant and she used her influence to share the gospel with as many people as possible. Over the school year, God used her to lead 16 students to the Lord! The harvest is plentiful on college campuses.

MY INFORMAL FIELD STUDY

We'll discuss the stigma that unbelievers have about Christians in chapter 4, but first let's discuss the stigma that many Christians have about unbelievers. Far too many Christians have bought into the idea that the harvest isn't plentiful. They may acknowledge that they're called to become fishers of men, but deep down they don't believe that the fish are still biting. That's not true. The real problem is that many in the body of Christ just aren't fishing. We're only reading books about fishing, or watching the fishing channel, or going to conferences about why the fish aren't biting in postmodern culture.

One piece of advice: Disregard any books or articles that say college students aren't open to the gospel. Many things have changed in culture, but the human heart hasn't. For nearly four decades, I've been conducting an informal field study. Our church has interviewed hundreds of thousands of college students on 50 campuses and we've also been in relationship with students from over 40 nations. Here's what we've discovered: Everywhere we go, 30-40% of college students are interested in learning more about the gospel. In other words, the fish are still biting!

MANY THINGS HAVE CHANGED IN CULTURE, BUT THE HUMAN HEART HASN'T

JUST START FISHING

Fifteen years ago, my dad, my three sons and I went fishing at a lake in northern Arizona. My dad and I started setting up our expensive new fishing equipment. As time passed, I thought to myself, "I'm gonna show my sons how to fish!"

While my dad and I were still setting up, my six-year-old son Caleb found a tangled three-foot fishing line with a rusty three-prong hook, and sat on some big rocks at the shoreline and started fishing. In 15 minutes, Caleb quickly caught not one, two or three fish, but four five-inch bass! This was all before my dad and I had even finished setting up our fishing poles! Then a fisherman about 100 yards away heard our cheering and yelled, "What's the kid using for bait?" Whimsically, I yelled back, "A tangled fishing line, a rusty hook and some initiative!"

That day, I learned an important lesson. You don't have

to know everything about fishing to catch fish. You just have to start fishing. In the same way, you don't have to know everything about evangelism and reaching college students, just start fishing!

WALK ACROSS THE CAMPUS

Years ago, two campus missionaries were meeting students at the University of Florida, starting conversations about faith, and sharing the gospel. After a long day of talking to students, they walked by the campus library, saw a girl on a bench smoking a cigarette, and went up to her to start a conversation.

The missionaries didn't know it then, but the student was tired of living for the weekend party scene. She felt empty inside and was starting to wonder, "Is this all there is to life?" As they talked, she sensed that something bigger was happening in the moment, like God was working in her heart. The missionary asked if she believed she would go to heaven when she died. She thought for a moment, and said she hoped so. He asked, "Why do you believe this?" Thinking as hard as she could, she said, "I hope the good things I've done in my life will outweigh the bad things."

Trying to help her understand the gospel, the missionary asked, "How many lies would you have to tell in order for me to call you a liar?" She answered, "I guess just one." Then he followed up, "So how many times would someone have to sin to be considered a sinner…" He didn't even have to finish the question. For the first time, she understood that she was a sinner. She went to a Bible study that same night and saw other students learning about God. Realizing it was possible to follow Jesus in college, she surrendered her life to Jesus.

That story happened almost four decades ago, and I'm indebted to those two campus missionaries because that girl is now my wife, Wendy! I'm so grateful for the campus missionaries who met Wendy that day.[12] Because they believed the harvest is plentiful, our family tree is forever changed. Trust me when I say I believe in personal witnessing and evangelism on college campuses, because not only was I reached on the college campus, but my wife was too.

SPEAKING AT A SEMINARY

A few years ago, I was asked to speak about evangelism at a seminary that I had previously attended. I told the professor I might step on some toes, but he still wanted me to come. Instead of doing a lecture, I brought students from our church to tell their stories of belonging and believing.

Ten students told their testimonies of how someone started a conversation with them on campus, asked them questions, listened, told their story and God's story, and how that led them to put the full weight of their trust in Jesus over time. The whole atmosphere in the classroom changed! The seminary students were shocked at what they were hearing because they had been convinced that college students weren't open to the gospel.

EVERYBODY'S OPEN SOMEDAY AND SOMEBODY'S OPEN TODAY

Like I said earlier, "Everybody's open to the gospel some-day, and somebody's open today." I've come to realize that the only way to get from *someday* to *today* is by sowing a ton of seeds (Psalm 126). It's easy to sow seeds when things are going well. It takes faith to sow when it's hard. There's rejection, people misunderstand us, it's inconvenient, and for those of us in Arizona, it's blazing hot outside. But like Phoenix Suns Coach Monty Williams says, "Everything you want is on the other side of hard."[13] When we sow seeds of friendship, connection, serving, and the gospel on our cam-puses and in the surrounding cities, we never know when an *everybody* will become a *somebody*.

WE NEVER KNOW WHEN AN EVERYBODY WILL BECOME A SOMEBODY

A STUDENT'S STORY

"At the beginning of my freshman year I met a campus mis-sionary and she invited me to church. I went a couple times but then I started ignoring her calls. I just wasn't ready to

think about spiritual things. Well, soon after, we ran into each other on campus. I told her I wasn't interested in church, so instead we started grabbing dinner together once a week. I could tell that she genuinely cared about me.

In the spring semester, I hit a low point. I'd done some things I wasn't proud of, and I remember crying out to God, asking Him to get me out of the pit I'd gotten myself into. Then, on the last weekend of the school year, this campus missionary invited me back to church. I knew immediately that God was answering my prayer. I went to Hope Church that weekend, heard the gospel and surrendered my life to Jesus. Later, I asked her what made her decide to invite me to church again. She said the Holy Spirit told her, 'Now is the right time.'"

– 19-year-old female student from Spring Valley, NV

Since 2010, our church has filmed more than 200 stories of students and graduates whose lives have been changed with the gospel. It's an ongoing project we call *Campus Changer Films*. If you're having trouble believing that the harvest is plentiful, take a minute to scan the QR code below and be encouraged by these young peoples' stories.

Now that we know the church should be on the offensive, we're all called to become fishers of men, and the harvest is plentiful, it's time to talk strategy.

CHAPTER SUMMARY

Scripture, firsthand experience, and research tell us that no matter what we think or feel, the fish are still biting on college campuses. Every college student is open to the gospel someday and somebody is open today.

Three biblical truths we need to embrace are:
- The church should be on the offensive.
- We're all called to become fishers of men.
- The harvest is plentiful on college campuses.

If we adopt these mindsets, we can win the Battle to Belong.

QUESTIONS TO CONSIDER

1. After reading this chapter, are there any ways that your ministry is on the defensive instead of on the offensive?

2. In your life and ministry, what would it look like to embrace the call to become a fisher of men?

3. Do you believe the harvest is plentiful on the campus you're reaching and how has that impacted the way you do ministry?

03
THE
STRATEGY

to win!

If we don't have a strategy, the enemy will.

D-DAY

On June 6, 1944, Allied troops approached the beaches of Normandy. Before them were five sectors of beach they wanted to use to establish a foothold against Hitler and his tyrannical rule. Guarded by mines, barbed wire, and guns positioned along the cliffs, the beach was heavily fortified with German defenses. The battle would be costly, but necessary.

With so much at stake, Allied generals knew they needed a holistic strategy. To increase the odds of success, the seaborne invasion was preceded by an airborne assault. They needed both *bombs in the air* and *boots on the ground* if they hoped to have any chance of winning. D-Day became the largest air, naval, and land operation in history, and the coordinated attack proved to be critical to the Allied forces' success and ultimate victory in the war.

WE NEED A STRATEGY

Just like D-Day was a critical battle that changed the momentum of World War II, winning the Battle to Belong is imperative to turning the tide on college campuses.

I think there's something we can learn from the Allies'

strategy on D-Day. Boots on the ground secured the victory, but it was the bombs in the air that paved the way for the ground forces to advance on the beaches. It's the same on college campuses. We need impact events that break the stigma about Christians (they're like bombs in the air). We also need authentic relationships to reach students individually, develop trust, and win their hearts (they're like boots on the ground).

WE ALSO NEED THE HOLY SPIRIT

Before I continue, let me make an important clarification. Yes, it's essential to have a solid, thoughtful strategy, but we need the power of the Holy Spirit even more. I love what Alpha International says about their ministry: "Alpha is perfectly designed to fail unless God shows up."[1]

When we look at the ministry of Jesus, we see that He was consistently strategic with His time (we'll talk more about that in a moment). But we also see that He was led and empowered by the Holy Spirit wherever He went. Acts 10:38 says:

You know of Jesus of Nazareth, how God anointed Him with the Holy Spirit and with power, and how He went about doing good and healing all who were oppressed by the devil, for God was with Him.

This combination of laser-focused strategy and complete reliance on the Holy Spirit led to tremendous impact.

MINISTRY IS A SUPERNATURAL JOB AND IT'S DESIGNED TO FAIL UNLESS GOD SHOWS UP ≪

This book will focus on the strategy of Jesus, but don't believe that a good strategy or a list of "best practices" is all we need to succeed. Ministry is a supernatural job, and it's designed to fail unless God shows up.

THE STRATEGY OF JESUS

As we look at the life of Jesus, we see that everything He did had a transcendent purpose and was tied to His overall mission: to seek and save the lost (Luke 19:10). There's no better book that better captures the DNA of Jesus's ministry than Robert Coleman's *The Master Plan of Evangelism*. Time and again, I return to this book to refresh myself and our leadership team with timeless truths from the ministry of

Jesus. In it, Coleman says, "His [Jesus'] life was ordered by His objective. Everything He did and said was a part of the whole pattern. It had significance because it contributed to the ultimate purpose of His life in redeeming the world for God. This was the motivating vision governing His behavior. His steps were ordered by it. Mark it well. Not for one moment did Jesus lose sight of His goal."[2]

Jesus implemented a similar strategy of impact events and authentic relationships. In fact, Jesus was all in to not just win the Battle to Believe, He was all in to win the Battle to Belong.

THE GREATEST IMPACT EVENT IN HISTORY WAS WHEN JESUS RESURRECTED FROM THE DEAD

IMPACT EVENTS IN THE GOSPELS

As we read the Gospels, we see that wherever Jesus went He shook up the culture with events that captured the crowd's attention. Do you remember when He fed 5,000 people with five loaves and two fish in Matthew 14:13-21? Or, when He walked on water in front of His 12 disciples in Matthew 14:22-33? Or, my personal favorite, when He turned water into wine at a wedding in John 2:1-11? What about when He raised Lazarus from the dead in John 11? That impact event was so revolutionary that afterwards the Pharisees plotted to kill Him!

And of course, the greatest impact event in history was when He was resurrected from the dead and later appeared to 500 people, at one time (1 Corinthians 15:6). Jesus put on impact events that caused people to say, "We have seen remarkable things today" (Luke 5:26).

But He didn't stop there.

AUTHENTIC RELATIONSHIPS IN THE GOSPELS

Throughout the Gospels, we see Jesus develop authentic relationships with all types of people. Jesus knew that if they spent time around Him, they'd learn His ways intimately. They'd learn to love what He loved and trust Him completely. And ultimately, many of them would follow His footsteps in giving their lives to reach the next generation.

Robert Coleman talked about this principle of building authentic relationships. He said, "Jesus didn't hold His disciples at a distance or remain behind a pulpit. He helped them belong by concentrating his time on a few men rather than the masses. He brought the disciples close to Him and explained in private why He did or said what he did. He invited them into His daily life, and everywhere He went, they followed. He actually spent more time with his disciples than with everybody else in the world put together."[2]

WE NEED BOTH

Impact events are like *bombs in the air.*
Authentic relationships are like *boots on the ground.*

Impact events are about *drawing crowds.*
Authentic relationships are about connecting with *individuals.*

Impact events produce *awe* and *wonder.*
Authentic relationships produce *trust* and *vulnerability.*

Impact events lead to *fun with no regrets.*
Authentic relationships lead to *friendships that last a lifetime.*

Impact events captivate people's *hearts and minds.*
Authentic relationships cultivate an *openness to the gospel.*

With both these key elements, we can win the Battle to Belong.

METHODS VS PRINCIPLES

It's been said, "Methods are many, principles are few. Methods may change, but principles never do." The Great Commission to go and make disciples will never change, and the gospel message never changes. But the most effective methods to reach the lost do change over time. Impact events and authentic relationships in today's world will probably look a little different from Jesus's day. The bottom line is, are we willing to do whatever it takes to reach college students and win the Battle to Belong?

Since the beginning of time, men have figured out ways to meet women and win their hearts. Think about it. A man will do whatever it takes to try and start a relationship with a woman he's interested in dating. So why can't we figure out how to meet lost people in a way that's appropriate? We can! I tell our leadership team to be creative, have fun, and think of how you would want to be engaged. Get out there and go for it.

Here's an example. When Northern Arizona University experienced a bunch of snow last January, our campus missionaries decided to make a snowman and put a jersey on it from their rival, Arizona State University. They stood 30 yards back and dared guys to hit the ASU snowman with a football. That day, they met 85 young men who were interested in coming to church or being in a Bible study. Now that's a creative way to say, "Come and see."

JESUS LIVED WITH URGENCY

As we look at the life and ministry of Jesus in the Gospels, we see that He lived a life of urgency. In fact, the word "immediately" is used more than 40 times in the Gospel of Mark. Scripture is clear that none of us are promised tomorrow, so He calls us to live with urgency today.

I believe there's something about living with urgency that pleases Jesus. Ecclesiastes 9:10 says, "Whatever you find to do with your hands, do it with all your might."[3] And Romans 12:11 NLT says, "Never be lazy, but work hard and serve the Lord enthusiastically."

Keep in mind, there's a difference between busyness and urgency. Busyness is just doing a lot of activity. Urgency is a focused mentality that leaves no room for excuses in answering three key questions:

- If not now… then when?
- If not here… then where?
- If not me… then who?

How does this relate to the college campus?

THE NEED FOR SPEED

Students want to make friends fast, and the friends they choose, especially in the first few weeks, set the course for the rest of their college careers. So, there's not a minute to waste. We need to move with a sense of urgency because if we don't have a strategy to connect with students as soon as they get to campus, the enemy will.

That's why our church puts an emphasis on meeting students at the beginning of the year. On average, we meet 7,000 students in the first two weeks and 12,000 students within the first six weeks. It's an all-hands-on-deck endeavor. And you know what? It's worth it, because this is the time when students are the most receptive to making new friends. And it builds momentum for the rest of the school year.

STUDENT EXPERIENCES

"The day I moved in at ASU I was standing in line, waiting to get the key to my residence hall, when I met someone from Hope Church. He was doing a survey to see what students wanted to get involved with on campus, and one of the options was a church. I had just gotten saved my senior year of high school, so I was looking for a church when I got to college. It turned out he was on staff with Hope Church so when I marked church on the survey, he invited me to come with him. I hadn't even been on campus for an hour yet and had already found a church. That's when I knew I was right where God wanted me to be."

— 18-year-old male student from Tucson, AZ

"My first day on campus, I met someone from Hope Church, but I wasn't interested in getting connected. I had given my life to Jesus when I was nine years old, but after some personal and family challenges, I walked away from my faith in high school and wanted nothing to do with God. I made the ASU football team my freshman year, and I thought I had it all together. But within a semester, I hit rock bottom. I started using and selling drugs, I was partying, drinking and cheating on my girlfriend, and before I knew it I had a 1.7 GPA and was suspended from the football team. I knew I need-

ed help. Fortunately, I remembered the guy from Hope that met me my first day at ASU. So I called him and asked to meet up. I opened up everything that was going on and he connected with me, encouraged, and showed me the truth. I needed to change. I needed to stop doing life my way and start following Jesus in college. So I repented and rededicated my life to Jesus and was immediately filled with hope."

– 19-year-old male student from Chandler, AZ

A BOBSLED RACE

Think about how crucial the start of a bobsled race is for everyone competing.[4] More often than not, the race is won or lost based on the initial push.[5]

The sled itself weighs about 400 pounds. For six seconds, athletes push the sled the length of about half of a football field (164 feet). As they push, they must overcome extreme resistance from static friction.[6] That first push is extremely difficult but each of the team members are "all-in" to do their part because they know that the momentum from the initial push will carry them for the rest of the race.

Just like Olympic bobsledders, how well we connect with students when they first arrive on campus will greatly influence our ministry's fruitfulness for the rest of the school year.

THE KEY

This combination of putting on impact events and building authentic relationships is the key to winning the Battle to Belong. It was the key to reaching people in Jesus's day, and I believe it's the same for us today. I'll share more about both these components in the following chapters.

CHAPTER SUMMARY

Winning the Battle to Belong requires more than a can-do attitude. We need a strategy, a sense of urgency, relentless creativity, and a desperate reliance upon the Holy Spirit. The strategy we see working is what Jesus Himself modeled: impact events and authentic relationships. Impact events are like bombs in the air and authentic relationships are like boots on the ground. And with this combination, we can win the Battle to Belong.

QUESTIONS TO CONSIDER

1. In what ways does your life and ministry align with the strategy Jesus had in the Gospels? Consider the principles of impact events, authentic relationships and urgency.

2. What could it look like for your ministry to invite unchurched students to "come and see"?

04

breaking the stigma on college campuses

IMPACT
MENTS

"Stigma beats dogma." – David French[1]

MY FIRST FRATERNITY PARTY

My first college fraternity party was unlike anything I'd ever experienced. Within moments, I was captivated by the allure of the college party culture. Alcohol, girls, and themed parties promised more fun than anything else on campus. And the truth is, I did have fun. Greek life tapped into something God put inside me as far back as I can remember.

As a child, I always enjoyed bringing people together. In grade school, I used to invite all the guys from Paradise Valley Day School to come together for epic squirt gun battles at the biggest backyards in the neighborhood. By the end of the day, the carnage looked like a Civil War reenactment. It was awesome. Even now, my favorite joke is that I like to be surrounded by 50 people all the time otherwise I start to get nervous. (Okay, maybe that is true.)

Students today are no different, whether they're extremely extroverted like me, or a little more introverted. Freshmen want to have fun and make friends fast, and Greek life is known for both. The brotherhood, sisterhood, and instant connections of Greek life make opportunities for fun nearly limitless. When you join, you become a member of an exclusive club, surrounded by dozens of peers and engaged all the time with events, activities, and parties. What's not to like?

Unfortunately, the same isn't often said about Christians on campus. A recent stat from Barna said 84% of non-Christians in their late teens and twenties have a negative impression of Christianity.[2] That's a staggering statistic that we have to take responsibility for. I'm not saying it's entirely our fault. After all, we have an enemy who accuses us day and night. But – can we at least take responsibility for our contribution to the problem?

FRESHMEN WANT TO HAVE FUN AND MAKE FRIENDS FAST

MAN LOOKS AT THE OUTWARD APPEARANCE

A well-known scripture in 1 Samuel 16:7 says, "man looks at the outward appearance, but the Lord looks at the heart." This passage is often used to help us understand that God is more concerned about our hearts than our physical appearance. However, years ago, my wife Wendy shared a different insight from this scripture that has stuck with me. She works with college women to develop personal style, tell them about the love of God, and explain how they're fearfully and wonderfully made. She points out that even though it's true that God looks on the inside, it's equally as true that man looks on the outside! Here's why this matters: If we don't care enough about our appearance, people may get the impression that we don't take our message seriously. On the other hand, if we're consumed with our appearance for our own ego's sake, people may get the impression that our appearance is more important to us than our message. But if our focus is to effectively reach a particular audience with our message, the goal should be to eliminate as many distractions as possible to maximize the clarity of our message. If we want to effectively reach people with the gospel, we have to care about what our audience is focusing on. The same truth should apply to our events.

Do we invite unsaved fraternity and sorority members to captivating events? What about the events we invite student athletes to, or student body leaders? Would they even want to come? And if they do, would they want to come back? If we asked for their feedback about the event, what would they say?

There's a stigma on college campuses that Christians are boring: they're not intelligent, not relatable, not relevant, not fashionable, and not fun. They're just NOT. The unfortunate reality is that we've contributed to that stigma and we can't blame anyone else. What if instead of getting mad at the next generation for their impression of us, we took responsibility for this perception and embraced what the Apostle Paul said in 1 Corinthians 9:22: "I have become all things to all men, so that I may by all means save some"?

I'm not talking about the endless pursuit of trying to appear cool or so relevant that we lose the ability to be salt and light. I'm talking about being so others-focused and intentional that we break through the negative impressions about Christianity long enough to get unsaved college students to attend our events. Not only that, but during the event we might capture their hearts and minds so much that they want to come back and bring their friends.

Let's not reinforce the stigma by throwing events that are just NOT. Let's break the stigma.

WITH UNLIMITED ACCESS TO THE CREATOR, WE CAN THINK BIGGER AND DO BETTER

BREAKING THE STIGMA

If we want to attract unreached and unchurched college students, we must break the stigma. As Christians, we should be the most fun-loving, lifegiving, and engaging people around. If we're serious about reaching lost people, the church should have the most incredible, excellent, and impactful events because we serve the living God who created the universe and rose from the dead. And with unlimited access to the Creator, we can think bigger and do better. No matter the size of our budget, it's possible to plan both small-scale and large-scale impact events that capture the hearts and minds of college students, give them an opportunity to connect with our communities, and compel them to explore their faith.

FUN WITH NO REGRETS

After I became a Christian, I noticed that the events my church was putting on weren't drawing students. Judging by the low attendance, other students didn't want to be there and I didn't want to be there or be seen there either! So, I asked if we could try something different and took some risks to see what might happen.

One time, I invited a former Wiccan witch to come and share her testimony in a residence hall lobby. It was an easy invite: Tell people they could meet a real witch. Around 90 guys from that residence hall came to hear her story, and I made the most of the opportunity to introduce myself and get to know them. Another time, we hosted a talent show, and while it might not have been *America's Got Talent*, it worked. Around 300 people came. Our team couldn't stop talking about how much fun we had, and how we must do it again. We did anything and everything to connect with college students. Everything was done with a desire to make friends with people who didn't know Jesus. Events, when done intentionally and thoughtfully, have the power to open doors to new relationships with the lost.

EVENTS HAVE THE POWER TO OPEN DOORS TO NEW RELATION- SHIPS WITH THE LOST

I brought this passion for fun when we planted Hope Church in 2004. I encouraged our leadership team to leverage their passions for the Great Commission and get creative. Over the years, our team has put on hundreds of fun-loving events, from small-scale to large-scale, casual to elaborate, house-to-house to a 3,000-seat auditorium designed by Frank Lloyd Wright. We've done "taco crawls" where we visit several local taco spots and rank them on taste, presentation, and value. We've put on weekly gym sessions (we call it "Friday Night Lifts") where we have a certified personal trainer coaching dozens of students as they lift weights in our church warehouse. We've done pop-up style workshops, where young women from campuses across Arizona learn how to develop their personal style. We've hosted the largest fashion show on a Pac-12 university campus. We've put on "Friendsgiving" dinners where our church movement rallies to host more than 1,000 students to bless them before they go home for the holidays. And one of my personal favorites is the "Flapjack Wagon," where we cook up fresh pancakes in the back of a truck and pass them out to hungry students during finals week. Not only do these events break the stigma on college campuses, but they show students it's possible to have fun with no regrets in college.

However today, our church movement's premier impact event is Survivor Weekend.

SURVIVOR WEEKEND

Picture this: it's Labor Day Weekend, the first three-day weekend of your freshman year. You've been recruited to a tribe of 200 other students from your residence hall and several others nearby. They want you on their tribe because they're competing against other tribes from more than twenty different college campuses. You all load up into charter buses. They're buzzing with energy because everyone's anticipating an adventure weekend of music, camping, and head-to-head competition. That's Survivor Weekend.

I like to describe Survivor Weekend as a mixture of the classic television show *Survivor*, the Spartan Race event, and Tough Mudder, with an EDM (Electronic Dance Music) concert thrown in. Students join tribes based on their location and campus, travel to northern Arizona, and compete against their peers from across the Southwest. Survivor Weekend has won awards for its excellence from one of the nation's largest universities but, more importantly, students form relationships that help them belong. These relationships last throughout their college years and beyond.

I wish Survivor Weekend existed when I was a freshman! No words can do Survivor Weekend justice, so scan the QR codes below to watch videos from our premier event.

Survivor
Highlight Video

Students' Feedback
from Survivor

STUDENT REACTIONS TO SURVIVOR WEEKEND

"You always hear people say something changed their life. But I actually think this is one of those events."

— 18-year-old male student from Los Angeles, CA

"It is so surreal that you're able to meet so many good people in such a small amount of time, and just make the best connections. Your tribe feels like your second family and you just met them. It's awesome."

— 18-year-old female student from Grand Rapids, MI

"When you come from high school and you're new to college, you don't know a lot of people. Most of the time you don't know what you're doing, you don't even know where

you are on campus. So having people you can bond with and trust and really talk with, that's amazing."

    – 18-year-old female student from Austin, TX

"It's my first Survivor Weekend, it definitely lived up to the hype. Better than the video!"

    – 18-year-old male student from Jacksonville, FL

NOT A CHURCH CAMP

Let me be completely clear: Survivor Weekend is not a church camp. It's an adventure weekend hosted by a collegiate-focused church.

For more than a decade now, Survivor Weekend has given thousands of students the experience of a lifetime, complete with face paint and plenty of mud. In addition to the fierce competition, on the second evening my wife Wendy and I share an inspirational message about how to thrive – not just survive – in college. In it, we encourage students to discover their "why" and to "choose their tribe before their trail." But here's what we don't do: we don't preach the gospel, play worship music, or have an altar call. That's not the purpose of the weekend.

Survivor Weekend is not about winning the Battle to Believe, it's about winning the Battle to Belong. It's open for anyone to come and exists to connect with students who are unchurched and give them a place to belong. Even if they never come to a Sunday service, we want to bless them with an unforgettable weekend and see them experience competition and community like they've never encountered before. That kind of impact event is compelling to college students and especially young men. In fact, 60% of the people who attend Survivor Weekend are young men.

A STUDENT'S STORY

"I remember freshman year and thinking I would do anything in my power for people to like me. I know the Bible says bad company corrupts good morals, and I saw that play out. I quickly got involved in the party scene, and then I felt like I had to keep going out and drinking in order to keep my friends and my boyfriend. I'd literally go out Saturday night and then come to church Sunday morning, trying to hide the fact that I was hungover.

Coming into sophomore year, I felt really lonely and like I needed to re-evaluate my friend group. I decided to go on Survivor Weekend, and it completely changed my life. All the people I met were having so much fun just being themselves, and I knew that was something I wanted too. I was sick of feeling pressured to compromise and trying to fit in. After the trip, with my new friends encouraging me, I started making some changes. I made some boundaries in my unhealthy friendships, and I started to develop deep relationships here at church! I tell all the girls I meet not to hesitate to come on Survivor - you'll form life-changing friendships in your tribe."

— 19-year-old female student from Yuma, AZ

STUDENTS FIND THEIR TRIBE, EVEN IF THEY AREN'T READY TO EXPLORE THEIR FAITH

IT'S A FAMILY AFFAIR

Because Survivor Weekend is a vital part of building momentum at the beginning of the school year, our whole church goes all in and all out. We even cancel our Sunday service that weekend because we want everyone engaged in winning the Battle to Belong. Everyone has a role. Students can lead on Survivor Weekend as Camp Guides. Their job description is simple:

- Have as much fun as possible
- Form friendships with your tribe
- Make sure no one gets lost in the woods

At the same time, college graduates and families lead and volunteer as "Survivalists." They referee games, serve meals, run the medic tent, take photos, and handle hundreds of other camp logistics (which is why we start planning this event in January each year). We couldn't put on this weekend trip without their hard work before, during and after the event. Just look at the 2022 highlights…

SURVIVOR WEEKEND 2022

10,000 meals
8,000 volunteer hours
1500 students and survivalists
250 tents
160-acre camp site
20 college campuses
8 tribes
1 trophy

It doesn't get more epic than that!

I hear stories all the time of students who come on Survivor Weekend and find their tribe, even if they aren't ready to explore their faith. These students will often continue connecting with our community long after the weekend is over. In fact, we've seen 70% of Survivor Weekend attendees visit a church service sometime during the school year.

SHAWN ROMO

One specific story that captures the heart of Survivor Weekend is the story of Shawn Romo. During Shawn's first three days as a freshman at Arizona State University, one of our church members met him and invited him to Survivor Weekend. After Survivor Weekend, Shawn continued connecting with his tribe, started exploring his faith and coming to church. Later that fall, Shawn surrendered his life to Jesus and began reaching his friends.

Everywhere Shawn went, he made new friends and invited them to join his tribe. As he developed friendships, he'd share his story and invite them to church. Shawn impacted dozens of students, and many started following Jesus because of his witness. Tragically, the summer before his junior year of college, Shawn passed away from an undiagnosed illness. He was 20 years old. Many students from Shawn's tribe attended his memorial service, and Shawn's parents were blown away. They soon learned that the hundreds of students they'd never met before were from Shawn's tribe at Survivor Weekend.

Shawn's legacy lives on today. We tell his story every year at Survivor Weekend and his parents join us to present the winning tribe with the coveted Romo Cup. On the side of the cup is a plaque with a photo of Shawn and an inscription that reads:

"In memory of Shawn Patrick Romo,
who found his tribe at Survivor Weekend,
built a culture of respect in college,
and left a legacy that won't be forgotten."

Watch this video to hear more of Shawn's story and the impact Survivor Weekend has had on his family.

HOW DO YOU PULL IT OFF?

At this point, you may be thinking, "That sounds amazing, but really expensive and elaborate... our team could never pull something like that off." I want to reassure you that Survivor Weekend didn't start as an impact event with 1,500 in attendance. It started as a dream and a ragtag group of our staff in 2011 who were willing to take a risk to connect with college students who didn't know Jesus.

That first Survivor Weekend, we took about 80 people up to the woods. We didn't have any custom-made games that mimic what you'd see on the television show *Survivor*. Instead, our team came up with simple games during the bus ride up. And you know what? More than 10 years later, there are still members in our church who got connected through that first Survivor Weekend.

It's not about how flashy or expensive your events happen to be. We all start somewhere. At the same time, we believe that putting on excellent events honors God and has the most impact, so we're dedicated to raising the money it takes to make events like Survivor Weekend affordable for college students to attend. I'll share more about fundraising in the appendix.

Overall, our hope is to produce impact events that capture the hearts and minds of college students and break the stigma on college campuses.

This isn't anything new; Christians have been doing that kind of thing for centuries.

TIMES HAVE CHANGED

Throughout history, Christians are the ones who have set the standard for excellence in culture. They've produced the best music, the best art, and the best architecture. In fact, as I've traveled around Europe the last few years, I've been able to witness firsthand some of the incredible art and architecture that has been designed by Christians. As we look back, it's clear that Christians like Johann Sebastian Bach[3], Michelangelo[4], and Charles-Édouard Jeanneret[5] helped set the standard for excellence in their fields.

Here's my question, when did the church stop setting the bar for excellence and leading in culture? Unfortunately, many times, because of a lack of creativity and excellence, Christians promote the stigma instead of leading the way and breaking the stigma. As Christians, our impact events should break the stigma and change the atmosphere around Christianity on our campuses.

KEY PRINCIPLES

When it comes to impact events, here are some principles we've learned over the years.

1. Look at the calendar

Nothing is worse than planning an event but nobody shows up because it's Homecoming Weekend at your university. As you plan your year, take a look at the calendar, including your university's academic calendar. Make note of key seasons, like midterms and finals, holiday weekends, and football games. As much as possible, plan your events with these in mind so students don't have to pick between your event and another competing priority.

2. Do something you love

Pastor Rick Warren says, "Write down what you love to do most, and then go do it with unbelievers. Whatever you love to do, turn it into an outreach."[6] If you aren't excited to be at your event, nobody else will be either. Our church loves competition and connection, so we created Survivor Weekend. We also love to laugh, so years ago we created Outlaw Comedy.

OUTLAW COMEDY

Have you ever noticed how laughter changes the atmosphere? That's how it was in my house growing up.

My dad was a great father to my brothers and me. He was also an accomplished medical doctor, so he was overall a studious and serious guy. The atmosphere in our house was typically serious, but when my dad would watch comedy and start laughing, the whole atmosphere would change. I think that's what Proverbs 17:22 talks about when it says, "A joyful heart is good medicine…" God created laughter to be good medicine for our souls. Here's the ironic thing – as a doctor, my dad would prescribe medicine to other people. But when he laughed, it was medicine to our family's souls.

Ever since I was young, I've been captivated by the

power of laughter and the gospel. In fact, when I was in seminary 15 years ago, I took all my credits and transferred from seminary to comedy school and I found out they were teaching the same thing! (And that was my first joke.) But seriously, here's what I love about comedy. When we laugh, the atmosphere changes, walls come down and everyone connects at a deeper level. I believe that's why our Outlaw Comedy shows have been so successful. Over the years, we've produced 52 shows with clean, but not cheesy, comedy for more than 30,000 students. Incredible talent like Bone Hampton, Ron Pearson and others have headlined our shows and even performed at our Sunday services. We consistently hear feedback from students about how much they love it.

Check out this highlight video from an Outlaw Comedy show:

A STUDENT'S STORY

"One day, I was sitting at a table in the dining hall telling a few friends, 'I don't see how being a Christian in college is gonna work'. Shortly after that conversation, a girl from

*Hope Church walked up to our table and invited us to go to
a comedy show. She was so confident and really friendly to
us, and for some reason I decided to go with her.*

*That comedy show was a ton of fun. It felt great to laugh
since I was feeling pretty discouraged. When I was there, I
could sense that something bigger was going on. I remember feeling like I had known these people for a long time,
even though I'd just met them. And that was so surprising to
me because I had hung out with the people on my floor all
year and still felt lonely.*

*Pastor Brian came up at the end of the show and said
that Hope Church put on this event to bless us with a few
laughs and he invited us to check out church if we ever
wanted to. I was floored that a church would go through
all that time and effort to connect with me. I knew I had to
check out what was going on Sunday."*

— 18-year-old female student from Ahwatukee, AZ

FASHION

My wife, Wendy, is passionate about personal style and
teaching women about their worth. So, over the years, our
church has hosted fashion shows and brought in world-
class speakers. In one of our favorite women's events, Pink
to Purpose, we invite a former Victoria's Secret Runway Angel to share her story of why she left the modeling industry.
According to the world's standards, she had it all: Money,
fame, and beauty. She shares vulnerably that those things
left her empty – and only the love of God can bring true

security and fulfillment. As you can imagine, her story captivates every woman in the room.

Watch a highlight video from one of our Pink to Purpose events:

STUDENT REACTIONS TO PINK TO PURPOSE

"We all think if I get this certain job, if I make this certain amount of money or fame, I'll be happy in life. But this event made me realize that sometimes God puts a certain void in us that only He can fill. This event really changed my whole perspective towards life."

— 18-year-old female student from Memphis, TN

"Just knowing that everything we see in the media is all fake, it makes me feel less pressure and it makes me think twice about the next time I want to compare myself to other women. God loves me just the way I am."

— 18-year-old female student from Reno, NV

"Jesus thinks I'm worthy, and I think that if I can display that, I can help other girls feel worthy too."

— 20-year-old female student from Fresno, CA

You don't have to do comedy shows and fashion shows, but you should do something that you and your team are excited about. Passion is contagious, and when people are excited to be there, they'll bring their friends too.

3. Be willing to pay the cost

Impact events aren't cheap. Great events take time, energy, and money. But it's worth it. Don't try to cut costs by sacrificing excellence. Keep the bar high.

We also must be willing to pay the cost with our time. Hosting impact events requires a great deal of planning. From finding a venue, to recruiting a leadership team, to setting up the event and tearing it all down, it's an investment. But it's worth it. And if we make the investment to produce an excellent event, we'll reap the benefits.

4. Be ready to follow up

We can produce the most incredible event in the history of our university, but if we don't follow up with the students who attend the event, we'll miss the opportunity to develop relationships that lead to the gospel. So, to follow up well, I recommend four things:

I.   **ASK FOR CONTACT INFORMATION.** Students that enjoy your event will often want to connect more with your community. So, it's important to have an appropriate way to collect contact information.

II. **HAVE A NEXT STEP.** What's the next thing you're inviting people into? You need a call to action at the end of every event, both from the stage and in personal conversations.

As an example, at our annual women's event, we do a plug for upcoming Bible studies focused on love, sex and relationships. We give time for students to scan a QR code, send us their feedback from the event, and select what future events they'd like to be invited to attend – including church and Bible study.

Here's another example. On the last day of Survivor Weekend, we give everyone a copy of our *Survivor Guide* and we invite them to join weekly groups for the next three weeks. The Survivor Guide is a values-based training we developed to help students throughout their college years. Chapter topics include being a "giver" versus being a "taker," how to develop your character, the importance of staying healthy, and leaving a legacy. It's a great way to continue building relationships with students who aren't interested in studying the Bible right away.

III. **FOLLOW UP QUICKLY.** You want to re-engage everyone within a couple days after the event, or the odds are high they won't remember why they gave you their number in the first place. We've discovered that in-person follow-up is the most effective way to build long-lasting relationships. So, in your follow-up plan, make sure it involves seeing people face-to-face.

BONUS TIP: When you're calling people to follow up with them after an event, stick to the three-attempt rule. If, after three attempts to contact an individual, they haven't responded, stop reaching out to them. The last thing you want to do is promote a negative stigma and drive people away from Christianity.

IV. **HAVE A LONG-TERM PERSPECTIVE.** The goal of any event is to build lasting relationships with guests who attend. I'll talk more about the importance of developing authentic relationships in the next chapter, but the best events pave the way for friendships to form. As an example, our Survivor Weekend event has a built-in structure for continuing relationships with students. They compete in their tribe throughout the weekend, eat together, campout, and forge bonds in the tug-of-war arena. They return from the woods, head back to campus, and continue to hang out with their tribe the rest of the school year. Tribes get together each week for parties, plan Friendsgiving dinners, throw study parties during finals, and more. It's an easy way to continue friendships with students who might not be ready for a church invite. Some people need to belong, before they believe.

CHAPTER SUMMARY

If we hope to reach unchurched students, there's a stigma about Christians on college campuses that needs to be confronted. Impact events do this effectively because they capture the hearts and minds of college students, give them an opportunity to connect with our communities, and compel them to explore their faith. All good things start small in the kingdom of God, so start with what you have, and students will see it's possible to have fun with no regrets in college.

QUESTIONS TO CONSIDER

1. Excellent events often cost time, money and energy. What typically prevents you from throwing great events? Discuss creative solutions with your team.

2. What do you love to do? What kinds of events (small- or large-scale) would you be passionate about hosting?

3. At your next event, how can you strategically develop relationships with students?

05

AUTHEN-TIC RELATION-SHIPS

guides who come alongside

*"They want a guide on the side
before they want a sage on the stage."*

– Tim Elmore[1]

COLORADO RAPIDS

Years ago, during a family vacation in Colorado, we went white-water rafting on the Arkansas River. We were cruising in Class 4 Rapids, and to put that in context, Class 6 Rapids are what you'd find at Niagara Falls. It was our first white-water rafting experience, so we didn't know much about navigating rapids. You could say that we didn't know what we didn't know. The river was fast, and full of powerful waves, rocks, eddies, and sharp turns. But even though we were completely inexperienced, we had an incredible time!

How did that happen? It was because we had a river guide in the boat with us. You see, if I had only read about white-water rafting or watched YouTube videos about it, that wouldn't have helped when we hit the rapids. Decisions had to be made quickly in the middle of dangerous waves, and only an experienced guide would've had the ability to do that. Thank God we had a person in the boat with us who knew what they were doing, because that river guide made all the difference.

It's the same way on college campuses.

GUIDES FOR THE RAPID RIVER OF SECULAR CAMPUS CULTURE

Every fall, millions of new students enter the Battle to Belong and the Rapid River of Secular Campus Culture at universities across the country. They leave the comfort, familiarity, and support of their families and find themselves surrounded by thousands of new faces. Just like I didn't know what I didn't know on the Arkansas River, students don't know what they don't know when they enter the Rapid River. It's their first time navigating it so they have blind spots, a limited perspective, and are rarely prepared for the monumental decisions they'll be forced to make in a short span of time.

At the beginning of every school year, I encourage students with the biblical truth that God knows, "the end from the beginning" (Isaiah 46:10). He knows exactly what's coming our way and the transitions we're navigating, so here's what He does: He sends us guides. A guide is someone who's already gone through the stage of life we're currently in and comes alongside us to help us navigate it successfully.

We see the concept of guides all throughout the Bible; here's just a couple examples. Almost 3,000 years ago, King Solomon, the wisest man who ever lived, apart from Jesus, talked about the importance of guides when he said, "He who walks with wise men will be wise, but the companion of fools will suffer harm" (Proverbs 13:20). Later in the New Testament, during one of the most important transitions in the Apostle Paul's life, God sent a guide named Ananias, into his life. I encourage you to read the whole story in Acts 9:6-16.

Even though Jesus spoke to the masses from time to time, He valued being a guide who came alongside. That's why He spent so much time with His disciples. He modeled the importance of spending time with people and developing relationships in such a way that it absolutely changed people's lives.

A JEWISH AGNOSTIC DRUG DEALER

My life changed my junior year through a very unlikely person – my fraternity brother, Ian. He was a Jewish agnostic drug dealer (which is a crazy combination!). One day, Ian walked into our fraternity house with a Bible. We all assumed it was hollowed out with a gun or drugs inside, but we soon found out that Ian was going to a Bible study led by a campus pastor. Soon after that, Ian surrendered his life to Jesus and his lifestyle radically changed. He stopped selling drugs, stopped partying, and most notably, he started treating women with respect. The changes in Ian's life sent ripple effects through our fraternity and had a profound impact on me.

At first, I was merely curious about what was happening to Ian. Then I was convicted because Ian was demonstrating that it was possible for someone to follow Jesus in college. Eventually, I was convinced. I knew that I had to either stop being Ian's friend, or I had to go all in with Jesus myself. I joined a Bible study with him, and I started going to church.

Up to that point in my life, my experiences with God, the Bible and Christianity were like my experiences in competitive swimming and water polo. Someone can be surrounded by 500,000 gallons of water and be dehydrated. In other words, it's possible to have water all around you but not inside you. It was the same for me spiritually. I had God's Word and truth around me, but I didn't have it inside me. As I began to read God's Word in a Bible discussion with Ian and a campus pastor, I started to realize just how spiritually dehydrated I truly was at the time.

Nine months later, at a church service, that same campus pastor spoke about water baptism. We looked at Romans 6:3-4, which describes baptism as a burial of the old life and I thought to myself, "Man, my life's a mess, I should get baptized." After the service, I went up to the pastor and asked if I could get baptized. He took me outside, and as the baptismal was filling with water, he asked, "Did you know it's illegal to bury a living person?" I laughed and said, "Yeah, everybody knows that." Then he looked me in the eyes and said, "So when did you die?" In other words, "When did you die to sin, self, and life lived on your own terms and put your faith in Jesus?"

I remember reciting all the religious things I was doing – my religious resume – but he interrupted me and asked, "How about now?" That's when the conversation went from personal to eternal. It was like God was looking right through his eyes at me. So, in that moment I decided to repent and put my faith in Jesus alone for my salvation.

Looking back, I'm eternally thankful for Ian, that campus pastor, and their friendship with me. Ian went against the flow in our fraternity and literally loved the "hell" out of my fraternity brothers and me. And that pastor was willing to ask tough questions that ultimately led me to put my trust in Jesus. Even though we were students, Ian became a guide when it came to my faith and helped me belong even before I believed. He went before me and showed how it was possible to follow Jesus in college. And then he came alongside me and walked with me. That's the power of authentic relationships.

SHOW AND TELL

Do you remember in grade school when it was *Show and Tell Day?* Everyone would bring something they thought was interesting to class and have a few minutes to describe it. Fortunately, my dad was in the Navy: he had a 15-month assignment in the Antarctic and brought back some interesting artifacts. The most impressive thing he brought back from his travels were five taxidermied baby emperor penguins. He gave one away to Harvard for research and one to the Woods Hole Oceanographic Institute. He gave a couple away to extended family and he kept one for our family.

I saw that penguin in our living room every single day. On Show and Tell Day in fifth grade, some of my classmates brought in things like popsicle stick forts, pet rocks, and, every now and then, there would be a living hamster or guinea pig. I couldn't wait for my turn. I'd proudly pull the penguin out from my bag and say, "Ladies and gentlemen, today for Show and Tell I present a baby emperor penguin."

Why is Show and Tell Day so fun as a kid? Perhaps it's

because it broke up the daily routine of listening to mundane lectures and experiencing predictable activities. We actually got to know our fellow classmates in a way the normal classroom environment didn't allow for. It gave us a window into what our friends were passionate about, what they thought was funny, and what their life at home was actually like.

Show and Tell teaches us that *people are more interested in a demonstration than an explanation.* When it comes to the gospel, most people are itching for a demonstration. Ian was a demonstration of the kindness of God and what it looked like to follow Jesus in our fraternity. It changed my life.

PEOPLE ARE MORE INTERESTED IN A DEMONSTRATION THAN AN EXPLANATION

THE KINDNESS OF GOD THROUGH HIS PEOPLE

Romans 2:4 says, "Do you think lightly of the riches of His kindness and tolerance and patience, not knowing that the kindness of God leads you to repentance?"

God doesn't draw us to Him through shame or condemnation but rather His kindness. One of the primary ways He does that is *through His people.* In the Gospels, Jesus promised that He would "build His church" and in the Book of Acts we see the church being built. In the Gospels, Jesus ministered through His physical body, and in Acts He ministered through His church body. I submit one of the ways people experience the "kindness of God" that "leads to repentance" is by building authentic relationships with other Christians. Jesus said in John 13:35, "By this all men will know that you are My disciples, if you have love for one another." I think it's safe to assume this can only happen when the church is in close proximity with lost people. We're called to be an extension of God's heart for a lost and broken world. As people sense the kindness of God through us, their walls will come down and we'll have an opportunity to share the gospel.

THE WRONG DECISION

One January, a freshman student was walking back to his Residence Hall after class when a campus missionary met him. They hit it off talking about sports, particularly football, and they exchanged phone numbers. The campus missionary asked him if he was interested in exploring his faith, and he said he had gone to church with his family as a kid, but hadn't been since he came to college. Over the next few weeks, the campus missionary invited him to play football with some of the guys and then to church on Sunday, but the student never got around to it. They would see each other on campus from time to time and he'd share how busy he was, but they never connected beyond that.

One year later, the campus missionary woke up to a text that said, "Hey man, I know it's been a while since we've talked. I wanted to see if you're still part of that church and if we could meet up." They grabbed coffee the next day and the student shared what had initiated the text. He said that when he met the campus missionary, he'd made a decision that set the course for the next year. Instead of getting involved with the church, he chose to join a social fraternity so he could party and hook up with girls. Over the next 12 months, his fraternity was kicked off campus, one of his pledge brothers died after a party got out of hand, and he was kicked out of the fraternity.

He told the campus missionary, "I'm in the same spot I was a year ago. I'm alone and I need to find some good friends. Last time I chose the party culture instead of the church and it was the wrong decision. This time I want to give the church a shot." Just one week later, the student surrendered his life to Jesus in a Gospel Appointment and later that semester, he was baptized.

KEY PRINCIPLES

Here's a few things we've learned over the years when it comes to authentic relationships.

1. Meet a ton of people and make a bunch of friends

That's our rally cry every fall. Fishermen know that if you don't have your pole in the water, you won't catch any fish. It's the same with meeting college students. Everywhere we go, we look for opportunities to meet new people. Whether you're standing in line at Starbucks, playing basketball at the rec center, cheering on your football team, or, whatever it is, you should keep your eyes open for who you can start a conversation with. You never know if the next person you meet is the person God wanted you to meet that day. We want to help students choose their people before their path and their tribe before their trail. In other words, we want to help them get connected with the right people, namely Christian community, so that they have a place they can belong before they believe.

EVERYWHERE WE GO, WE LOOK FOR OPPORTUNITIES TO MEET NEW PEOPLE

2. Pray for them

Nothing happens apart from the power of the Holy Spirit. We can meet as many people as we want, but if God doesn't move in people's hearts, it won't lead to changed lives. That's why prayer is so important. Our prayer strategy begins over the summer, when members of our church sign up to walk around the campuses we're reaching and pray for the students that will move in that fall. We call it *72 Circles*[2] for two reasons. First, because we're praying for God to move in the first 72 hours that freshmen get to campus. Second, because we complete 72 prayer circles in total. Not only do we launch the school year with prayer, but throughout the semester we have weekly prayer meetings we call *Fight Night*, where our church comes together to fight in the Spirit through worship and prayer to see God move.

We also encourage our members to make a list of friends they want to reach and pray for them individually throughout the week. This is a practice I started doing back in college. I'd write down the names of my friends and fraternity brothers, and start praying for them. At first nothing seemed to happen – but as I continued to pray, God began orchestrating divine appointments. I'd run into them on campus, and they'd eventually come to church or a small group. Some of them even surrendered their lives to Jesus while we were in college. Others became Christians five, ten, 15, even 20 years after we graduated. There's power in persistent prayer!

3. Remember their names

All of us have a desire to be valued and recognized as individuals, and nothing makes us feel that way like someone remembering our name. Your name is a unique marker that represents who you are. When someone remembers your name, they're communicating something about your value to them.

I can't stress this enough. Remembering someone's name is more than a skill to be learned; it's essential to developing authentic relationships. It's a value of our ministry and something that characterized the ministry of Jesus. In John 10:3, Jesus said that the good shepherd "calls his own sheep by name and leads them out." Remembering someone's name is critical to building trust with them, and it's a simple way to show them that they matter to you.

HILLARY'S STORY

"I was a junior in college and had just surrendered my life to Jesus when my friend brought me to a Hope Church service. But this wasn't my first time at Hope. God had been putting people in my path all throughout college, so I had actually visited Hope two years earlier when a classmate invited me.

After service, my friend said he wanted to introduce me to Wendy (Pastor Brian's wife), but he didn't know that we had met before. As we walked over to meet her, I kept thinking, "She's not going to remember me. It's been two years. I look completely different. And I'm sure she's met thousands of students since then." But when she turned around to shake my hand, she looked me in the face, smiled, and said "Hi Hillary, it's so nice to see you again!"

Immediately I felt known and loved. And God used that moment to speak to my heart that this was the church family He was placing me in."

KNOWN, LOVED AND CHALLENGED

Pastor Matt Keller from Next Level Church highlights three things that, deep down, every one of us is looking for: We all want to be known, loved, and challenged.[3] People feel known when we remember their names, ask them questions, and take time to get to know them deeper. Then, as we build friendship with them, our hope is that they'll experience the love of God through us. As people feel known and loved, there will be opportunities to challenge them to grow in their faith. Challenging someone is simply "encouraging them beyond their current comfort level."

We don't just need to be known, loved, *or* challenged, we need all three.

4. The 101% Principle

> "Birds of a feather flock together."
> "They're like two peas in a pod."

It's true, some people naturally connect well together. Similar backgrounds, shared interests or passions and certain personality traits can draw us together with someone naturally. Other times, it may be difficult to relate. But God calls us to connect with all different kinds of people. In 1 Corinthians 9:22 the Apostle Paul said, "I have become all things to all men, so that I may by all means save some." In other words, Paul did whatever it took to relate and connect with whoever he was with at any given time.

How do we do that practically? Social scientist Tim Elmore says to follow the 101% principle. Find the 1% you have in common and give it 100% of your attention.[4] If you both like to eat French fries, do a taste test to find the best fast-food French fries on campus. If you both love to play football, set up a time to throw the ball around and introduce the person to some of your other friends. If all you have in common is that you both have hair on the top of your head, take the person to get a haircut. And if you don't have hair, use the money you're saving and take them to get a haircut anyway. Find something! Anything! And then put 100% of your effort into connecting around it.

One of our campus missionaries met a student who was a self-proclaimed atheist several years ago. The student had a lot of walls up and was difficult to connect with at the time. But this campus missionary was determined to befriend her. The only personal thing she knew about her was that she was a criminal justice major. So, the campus missionary stepped out on a limb and asked if she liked true crime shows. Fast forward a couple days and they had watched multiple documentaries together about various criminal trials throughout history. That campus missionary found the 1% to connect over and I'm happy to share that the effort to connect with that student paid off eternally. That student surrendered her life to Jesus.

5. Play Chess, Not Checkers

Checkers is a simple game. Every piece is the same: They look the same, they move the same, and they all have the same goal. On the other hand, chess is way more complex because every piece is different. The knight moves differently than the bishop, which is different from the rook. Every piece must be treated uniquely.

We're playing chess when we form friendships on campus. Every student we encounter is unique and developing authentic relationships requires a personalized approach.[5] Remember, not everyone is receptive to the gospel when we first meet them. Some are more open to connecting with us than others, so we have to use discernment to know how to take the next step in every relationship.

Here are two simple questions to ask when it comes to reaching students:

1. What does this person need?
    Does this person need help with anything? Maybe they need help with their time management, goal setting, their exercise routine, or maybe they simply need a ride to the grocery store to buy some groceries.

2. What is this person's speed?
    In other words, are they on the fast-track to following Jesus? Or are they taking it a little slower? Whatever it is, we need to be aware so we can serve students effectively.

This is the art of building authentic relationships. I wish there was a scientific formula that could tell us exactly where someone is at, but, unfortunately, there isn't. Like farmers inspecting their crops to determine when to harvest, we must be sensitive to each relationship, ask questions to gauge their receptivity, and be led by the Holy Spirit to know how to relate appropriately.

RECEPTIVITY SPECTRUM

In my early years of campus ministry, the team that I was on developed a tool that has proven to be helpful over the years. It's called the Receptivity Spectrum. Here's how it works:

RED	YELLOW	GREEN
Hostile or Resistant	Cautious or Indifferent	Interested or Receptive

GREEN – GO

If you meet someone on campus who's interested or receptive in having a relationship with you and they also give you their contact information, they're a green. Green means go! They're open to friendship, so move forward with engaging them and investing in the relationship.

YELLOW – SLOW DOWN / BE CAUTIOUS

If someone gives you their information, but they seem cautious or indifferent, they're most likely a yellow. Yellow means proceed with caution. Look for opportunities to connect, but don't push it too much. Be strategic about what you invite them into.

RED – STOP / LEAVE THEM A FRIEND

If someone is resistant to having a relationship with you – or they may seem politely interested, but they don't give you their contact information – then they're a red. Red means stop. They aren't open, so don't follow up with them. If you see them on campus, wave and be friendly, but don't try to have a long conversation.

This spectrum helps us connect with people appropriately and serve them the best way possible. And here's the thing, we must re-evaluate this every week because people's receptivity changes over time. As an example, someone might be hesitant to explore faith, but then they hear someone's testimony and become more interested in hearing the gospel. Or maybe someone originally said they wanted to come to a Bible study, but after a couple weeks they stopped responding to phone calls. And when people hit a crisis, their receptivity can change dramatically. So, we always must be ready to adjust our plan accordingly.

The receptivity spectrum isn't the "be-all and end-all" of ministry. It simply gives us a way to gauge how open a student is to the gospel so that we can prioritize our time and reach out to those who are receptive. We want to spend the most time with the people who want our ministry.

LONGEST DISTANCE BETWEEN TWO POINTS

I'll close this chapter by addressing two things. First, there's a tendency in all of us to take shortcuts, but building relationships takes a lot of time. Like John Maxwell says, "the longest distance between two points is a shortcut."[6] There's no shortcut for learning someone's name, getting to know them, and building trust. There's also no shortcut for praying for your friends and evaluating their receptivity so you can relate appropriately.

That's why, in our church movement, each of our full-time staff spends 30 hours a week physically on campus developing authentic relationships. They take time to plan and prepare for the week, but then they go to campus because that's where the students are at. The only way to develop authentic relationships is by spending time with people. So make the investment with your time and don't try to take shortcuts.

IT TAKES ALL GENERATIONS TO REACH THE NEXT GENERATION

Second, some people think that they can't reach college students because of their age or stage in life. While I firmly agree with missiologists that the best people to reach a specific people group are the indigenous people themselves (in other words, the best people to reach college students are college students), I also believe that it takes all generations to reach the next generation.

Psalm 145:4 NLT says, "Let each generation tell its children of Your mighty acts; let them proclaim Your power."

130

And Psalm 78:4 NLT says, "We will not hide these truths from our children; we will tell the next generation about the glorious deeds of the LORD, about his power and his mighty wonders." Scripture makes it clear that when it comes to reaching the next generation, we all have a role to play.

I've seen the power of a multi-generational church reaching college students. While the majority of our church members are college students or young graduates in their 20s and 30s, we also have a growing number of families with children, Gen Xers like myself, and even some members in their 70s and 80s. Never underestimate the power of young professionals sharing their testimonies and encouraging students, or married couples mentoring dating couples, or families having students over for a home-cooked meal. It's simple but profound. Students need to connect with older generations who have gone before them to give them wise counsel and hope that they can make it, too.

When I was a student, there was a family that invited me into their home for dinner. After eating a home-cooked meal, the father brought me to his shed in the backyard. (I thought he was gonna kill me!) When we got there, he gave me a painting. I'll be honest, he wasn't an incredible artist, but the fact that he cared enough to give me one of his paintings had a profound impact on me. I even hung that painting in my room. I've never forgotten how much that meant to me as a student, to be invited into their home for dinner and to be shown that kind of genuine love and care.

GRACEPOINT CHURCH

My friend and gospel-hero, Pastor Ed Kang (from Gracepoint Church) has modeled this extremely well. Gracepoint's church movement currently reaches 70 campuses in 40 cities, and they describe themselves as "fueled by 1,600 co-vocational ministers."[7] It's incredible what God has done through their ministry. And a large part of that is because they have a multi-generational church. After students graduate, they find jobs in the marketplace and devote hours each week to connect with students on campus, lead Bible studies, serve the surrounding community and host students at their homes for home-cooked meals.

So, whether you're single, married, married with kids, or even a grandparent like me, you can help reach college students. Invite students into your home and see how God uses that to minister to them. I like to say if you can get people into your house, you can get them into God's house.

CHAPTER SUMMARY

Students aren't primarily looking for a sage on the stage. They're looking for guides to come alongside them. It doesn't matter if you're an upperclassmen, graduate, young couple, family or even a grandparent like me, we can all build authentic relationships with students and help them feel known, loved, and challenged. Let's not hesitate to pray for students, invite them over to our homes and get to know them, because as we do, we'll help win the Battle to Belong.

QUESTIONS TO CONSIDER

1. Building authentic relationships often costs us time and energy. What typically prevents you from knowing, loving and challenging college students?

2. In your ministry context and stage of life, what can you do to develop meaningful relationships with college students?

3. Who are five students you're praying for and building relationships with right now? Make a list and add every student you know. If you don't know any, how can you meet or be introduced to some?

06
ACTION TRUMPS EVERY-THING

not easy but worth it

*"The one thing we can't do [in heaven] that
we can do here is tell people about Jesus."*

– J.D. Greear[1]

THE WAR MACHINE

Throughout the 1930's, America was struggling with the worst economic depression the country had ever experienced. On top of that, our nation was still recovering from the pain and catastrophic destruction from World War I, also known as The Great War. At that point, many Americans were inclined to avoid another world war at all costs and as a result, they ignored the growing threat from Germany, hoping that their aggression would simply go away. But it didn't. Those Americans were known as isolationists because they isolated themselves from the conflict and didn't want to get involved overseas. And with the war happening in Europe, they didn't think it would impact them personally. But when Japan bombed Pearl Harbor, everything changed. Suddenly, we couldn't ignore the fight anymore. The fight came to us, and America went to war. President Roosevelt began to rally our country, and everyone got to work. Every American – even grandmothers – were mobilized to contribute to the war effort.

    Then President Roosevelt did something that changed

the war and the United States forever. He mobilized businesses to ramp up the war machine. Instead of making cars, companies like Chrysler, Ford, and General Motors started making tanks and planes. The average Ford car had 15,000 parts, whereas the B-24 Liberator Long Range Bomber had more than 450,000 parts. And get this, one bomber came off the line every 63 minutes.[2] Now that's a nation on a mission! Once America stopped ignoring the fight and took action, we helped defeat Adolf Hitler and the Axis Powers. Because everyone did their part, we won the war.

I share that story because the Battle to Belong is way bigger than a world war, it's an eternal war. And God is rallying and recruiting people at every age and stage to contribute to the war effort and help win the next generation on college campuses. It's not the time to sit on the sidelines like an isolationist, hoping the war goes away and doesn't involve us. Now is the time to rise up and get in the fight. Yes, we need vision. Yes, we need passion. But more than anything, we need action because action trumps everything.

YES, WE NEED VISION. YES, WE NEED PASSION. BUT MORE THAN ANYTHING, WE NEED ACTION. ≪

TAKE THE BATON

Because Jesus loved the world so much, He was never content to sit on the sidelines. He moved toward the lost, He moved toward the broken and moved toward the sick. And while Jesus isn't here on earth anymore, God is still moving through His people, the church. Now it's our turn. God wants to move through us, but we must take the baton.

Speaking of batons – can we talk about the US men's 4x100 Olympic relay teams? They've messed up or dropped the baton exchange at eight out of the past 12 Olympics and World Championship meets. It's terrible to watch the baton get dropped during the Olympics. But think about how much worse it would be if we don't take the baton of the gospel in our generation.

INTENTIONALITY

There's something we must know before we take the baton. We're going to face resistance. Make no mistake, our spiritual enemy is very intentional about destroying the lives of college students. In fact, his job description is to "steal, kill, and destroy" (John 10:10). So, if we're gonna take the baton and rescue the next generation, we must be intentional too. When Jesus was on earth He was strategic and intentional. If the devil is intentional about deceiving and destroying, we must be intentional about declaring the truth and rescuing. Sometimes that intentionality is mistaken for pushiness, but I'd prefer to err on the side of taking godly risks than to live afraid of accusation and sit on the sidelines.

ACTION BRINGS RESISTANCE: THE PHYSICS OF THE GOSPEL

We all learned Newton's First Law of Motion in high school physics class, that an object in motion tends to stay in motion and an object at rest tends to stay at rest. I've learned the same is true when it comes to the gospel. Follow me here.

In Matthew 28, we see the Great Commission where Jesus said, "All authority has been given to Me in heaven and on earth. Go therefore and make disciples of all the nations…" After Jesus reminded the disciples about His authority, He said "go" – which suggests the Great Commission is all about motion. I like to say: *A Christian in motion tends to stay in motion but a Christian at rest tends to find fault and accuse other Christians in motion.* Now when I say, "Christians at rest," I'm referring to Christians who are silent about their faith and not moving toward the harvest. When they see other Christians on the move, they're either convicted to start moving, or they'll try to stop the momentum because of their own discomfort. It's a sad reality that some of the most intense opposition we face can be from within the church itself.

PERSECUTION WILL COME

In the landscape of college campuses, many faculty and staff don't have a Christian worldview and don't understand the Great Commission. And since people tend to be skeptical of things they don't understand, Christian groups who are "on the move" often receive derogatory labels. Some of the most impactful ministries and collegiate-focused church-es that are changing the world for Christ have been misla-beled as aggressive, pushy or the ultimate dirty word, a cult. This isn't anything new. In fact, 2,000 years ago, when Paul arrived in Rome, Jewish leaders told him they didn't know much about Christianity, only that it was "spoken against everywhere" (Acts 28:22).

Now the truth is that no one does ministry perfectly. We've made our share of mistakes over the years, and we take feedback very seriously. When you have a very young church (average age 23 years old) including lots of new dis-ciples and recently graduated staff members, mistakes and misunderstandings are bound to happen. Young Christians tend to have a lot of zeal but can lack wisdom – so out of their passion, they can make mistakes. That's why as a col-legiate-focused church planting movement, we greatly value feedback to help us train our staff members more effectively. We want to do our best to train our team to use discernment and wisdom in all of their interactions with students.

As Peter said in 1 Peter 3, "If you suffer for doing what is right, God will reward you for it. So don't worry or be afraid of their threats." Let's take Peter's advice and not be con-cerned with being persecuted for doing what is right: serving people, sharing the gospel, and sharing the truth in love. And at the same time, let's not cause unnecessary perse-cution because we're offending people or breaking rules un-necessarily. Some of the biggest mistakes I've made in min-istry were because I wasn't self-aware and using wisdom in presenting myself to students.

THE FIRST CHURCH

In scripture, we see that the first church didn't let fear of persecution prevent them from fulfilling the Great Commission. In the beginning of Acts, everything started off great: Jesus ascended, the Holy Spirit descended, the disciples started sharing the gospel and thousands of people got saved. Miracles were happening all around them, and they started changing their city and beyond for God's Kingdom.

But then the switch flipped, and things got hard. They received all kinds of accusations, from both religious leaders and government officials. They were arrested and beaten. Opposition arose and various haters did whatever they could to shut down their ministry. As things became harder for the first church, notice what they did and didn't pray about. They *didn't* pray for God to take them out of the tribulations and persecution. Instead, in Acts 4:29, they prayed for God to give them boldness and courage in the middle of it. And in Acts 5, after Peter and the apostles were arrested, it says:

The apostles left there rejoicing, thrilled that God had considered them worthy to suffer disgrace for the name of Jesus. 42 And nothing stopped them! They kept preaching every day in the temple courts and went from house to house, preaching the gospel of Jesus, God's Anointed One! (Acts 5:41-42)[3]

That's who God has called us to be: An unstoppable church on the move, just like in the book of Acts. The first church never stopped taking action – and the same should be true for us.

THE FIRST CHURCH NEVER STOPPED TAKING ACTION – AND THE SAME SHOULD BE TRUE FOR US !

CHANGE OUR WORLD

The first church changed the known world. It's generally agreed by historians that Christianity went from a few dozen followers in 30 AD to six million by 300 AD, and by 350 AD there were more than 30 million Christians.[3] I believe God wants to do a similar thing today. He wants to change the world with the gospel. But to change the world, we must change college campuses because that's where the future leaders of our cities, our nation and our world are at.

Think about it:
- When we reach a young woman, we could be reaching a future wife and mother.
- When we reach a young man, we could be reaching a future husband and family.
- When we reach a political science student, we could

be reaching a future elected official.

- When we reach a business student, we could be reaching a future business owner or leader in a company.
- When we reach an elementary education student, we could be reaching a future teacher or university professor.
- When we reach an international student, we're one step closer to winning their country for Christ.

Reaching college students is the adventure of a lifetime. It's not easy, but it's worth it. When we go all-in to reach college students, it's the greatest investment we can make because the potential return is greater than we could ever imagine. If we win the Battle to Belong (and ultimately the Battle to Believe) on college campuses, our culture will change in profound ways.

REACHING COLLEGE STUDENTS IS THE ADVENTURE OF A LIFETIME.

SAVE THE SINKING BOAT

I want you to consider this illustration. Our culture is like a sinking boat. Just watch the evening news, and you'll see every day there's something new that reminds us of a different crisis or challenge we're up against.

When someone is in a sinking boat, they only have two options:

1. They can bail the water out from the top of the boat, one bucket at a time.
2. Or they can plug the hole at the bottom of the boat.

Spiritually speaking, what does it look like to bail water out from the top? That's when we focus on reaching people with the gospel after college. We provide counseling for failed marriages and recovery programs for addicts. We host financial seminars to become debt-free. We visit inmates in prison and try to help the homeless in our cities. Now don't get me wrong, those ministries are necessary and meet a need in our communities, but they don't solve the root problem. Remember, only 3% of people get saved after the age of 30 years old.

Instead of bailing water out from the top, I recommend that we plug the hole at the bottom of the boat by winning the Battle to Belong on college campuses.

Consider what would happen:

- If everyone reading this book was committed to treating college students as the most strategic unreached people group?
- If we all committed to praying fervently for the incoming freshmen class on campuses near us?
- If we were passionate about producing small-scale and large-scale impact events that break the stig-

ma and capture the hearts and minds of college students?

- If we were all in to build authentic relationships and be guides who came alongside students during the most critical time in their lives?

I believe that the spiritual climate of our cities, nation, and world would radically change. And as the next generation begins turning to God and seeking His face, He will heal our land (2 Chronicles 7:14). The next generation of college students are depending on us to take action.

Will you do your part to win the Battle to Belong?

CHAPTER SUMMARY

The Battle to Belong is way bigger than any world war. It's an eternal war. Now is the time to rise up and get in the fight. We're here because more than 2,000 years ago the disciples took action and decided to spread the gospel to the world. This movement changed world history and has impacted the lives of millions of people for eternity, and now it's our turn to take the baton. While reaching the college campus, we will undoubtedly experience resistance and even persecution, but Jesus has called us to be an unstoppable church on the move. The first church never stopped taking action and the same should be true for us.

Let's take the baton and change the world.

QUESTIONS TO CONSIDER

1. In what ways does your church follow the model of the early church in Acts? In what ways does it not?

2. What is the next step you can take to get in the battle?

3. How many students in your ministry did you win to the Lord? What steps can you take to see this number increase?

APPENDIX

Here are some frequently asked questions I've received over the years:

1. All this sounds awesome, but expensive. How do you raise enough money?

A lack of resources is one of the most common obstacles preventing ministries from effectively reaching college students. Impact events take resources and so does building authentic relationships. But we should never let a lack of resources prevent us from reaching the lost. We serve the living God and He owns the cattle on a thousand hills (Psalm 50:10 NLT), so there's no lack of resources in God's economy. I love what John Bevere said in his book *Killing Kryptonite,*

> "Jesus promises that when we seek first His kingdom and His righteousness, everything we need will be given to us. Not once did a lack of resources keep Jesus from doing what He needed to do … when we let the pursuit of God's kingdom possess us, He entrusts us with the necessary possessions to advance His will on earth."[1]

Once we believe that God can and will provide all the resources we need, we need a plan to raise the money. Over the years we've raised millions of dollars to resource our efforts to reach students in the Battle to Belong, and there are two primary lessons we've learned.

Money follows vision.

I love how my friend Steve Shadrach puts it in *The God Ask,* "People give to people – justified by a cause."[2] If you need to raise money to help you reach college students, don't just tell people about your need. Tell them about your vision and invite them to play a part in it.

Every year we do a partnership event called *Vision Sunday* where our church invites family members, friends, and ministry support partners to come hear the vision for the coming year. We share about the Battle to Belong, show videos of students' stories, and invite everyone to join us by partnering financially. And every year, God provides.

Here's an example video from a Vision Sunday event. (All of our videos are produced in-house by a team of students and graduates.)

Get creative.

Sometimes God uses unconventional means to provide. For example, in the Old Testament, God caused manna to fall from heaven and water to spring from a rock when the Israelites were in the wilderness. Then, in the New Testament, Jesus fed 5,000 people with just five loaves and two fish. Talk about unconventional provision. That's the same God we serve today. He's still meeting every need we have, but sometimes He wants to do it in a unique way to show that He's our provider. I remember years ago, we were hosting a comedy show to welcome the freshman class to campus. We had an opportunity to have the show at Grady Gammage Auditorium, a 3,000-seat theater on the ASU campus, but we needed $50,000 to pay for it. So we prayed and asked God for a miracle. That same day, a university administrator shared about a recycling program they were starting that needed student volunteers to help at sporting events. They would pay us the money we needed if our students were willing to volunteer. It was a miracle. God creatively provided exactly what we needed to reach thousands of students.

Winning the Battle to Belong is costly. But if we remember that money follows vision and we get creative, we'll see God come through. He doesn't want a lack of resources to keep us from reaching the lost - He's more passionate about reaching the lost than we are.

2. Meeting thousands of students sounds exhausting. What keeps you motivated?

On average, our team meets 7,000 students during the first couple weeks of school, and over 800 students in a typical week throughout the rest of the school year. If we don't see much fruit right away, it can be discouraging. I believe that's one of the tactics the enemy uses to try and get us to stop moving toward the harvest. We have to overcome discouragement and keep moving forward.

One of the anchoring passages I always come back to is Psalm 126.

> When the Lord brought back the captive ones of Zion
> We were like those who dream.
> Then our mouth was filled with laughter
> And our tongue with joyful shouting;
> Then they said among the nations,
> "The Lord has done great things for them."
> The Lord has done great things for us;
> We are glad.
> Restore our captivity, O Lord,
> As the streams in the South.
> Those who sow in tears shall reap with joyful shouting.
> He who goes to and fro weeping, carrying his bag of seed, shall indeed come again with a shout of joy, bringing his sheaves with him.

As an evangelist, the promises in verses five and six are some of my favorites in the whole Bible. Before there's sowing and reaping, there's sowing and weeping. That's because sowing seeds is hard work and we can easily become tired or discouraged. But look at the promise: if we keep moving forward, we'll see sheaves. Sheaves are the bundles of wheat that farmers gather during harvest. If we're planting seeds of the gospel, the sheaves are souls won to the Lord. And with that joy set before us, we can endure or face any challenge.

Another key is to mobilize members of your church to pray for your team and for college students. Older members may not be on campus meeting students, but they *can* and *should* get involved through prayer.

3. How do you get leaders bought in to spend that much time and effort doing outreach?

I regularly remind our team of our mission and vision. No matter how long we've done this, we always have to remind ourselves why we're doing it in the first place. I've heard that vision "leaks" every 28 days, and when vision leaks, people can get discouraged or begin to complain. The importance of vision can't be stressed enough. Scripture even says that without vision, the people perish (Proverbs 29:18).

We also take time to celebrate. Celebrating the who and what of ministry gives our leaders a fresh vision, especially in busy seasons. We're partnering with God to work in the harvest, so we want to celebrate what God is doing in the small things as much as the big things. Don't minimize the impact of presenting something like a "Servant of the Month" award, or thanking your leaders publicly. In fact, every week, at our Sunday services, we celebrate stories of salvation, transformation and outreach by watching Campus Changer and City Changer stories. We firmly believe that whatever we celebrate, we will reproduce.

4. What is your strategy when you initiate conversations with students on campus? Do you ask them spiritual questions or tell them about your next event?

I was first introduced to Dr. Rice Broocks when I was a college student and I consider him to be one of the greatest evangelists of our generation. He developed the S.A.L.T method of evangelism which we use to train our team to engage new students.[3] S.A.L.T. is an acronym that stands for:

Start conversations
Ask questions
Listen
Tell your story and God's story

This simple method has helped us train hundreds of students and graduates to reach others. We typically equip our teams with questions that lead the conversation into spiritual topics (e.g. What's your faith background? Have you thought about exploring faith in college?), but we also look for opportunities to connect over other interests throughout the conversation. Our goal is to find something to connect about, and if we have an event coming up, especially one of our big impact events, we'll invite people to join us.

We want to have both tools in our belt (S.A.L.T. and up-coming events) so we're equipped to connect appropriately with anyone we meet.

5. How do you follow-up with that many students after meeting them in their first few weeks on campus?

Meeting new students is where the job begins. Following them up is the most important part because we want to build relationships, not just meet a ton of people. The key is to see them in-person again as soon as possible. In order to do that, we need three things:

First, we need permission to follow them up. We don't want to follow up if someone doesn't want it. That's why whenever we meet someone we ask them if they want us to reach out to them about events and other activities we're doing.

Second, we need something to invite them to. This could be grabbing lunch, going to the gym, having a hangout at a house nearby, or even going to an event on campus. It can be anything - so long as it's something we think they'd be interested in.

Third, we need time in our schedule dedicated to reaching out to the people we've met. The best case scenario is to set up a time to connect when we first meet them. More often, we need to reserve time to follow up and schedule meetups. One general pattern is to start the day meeting new people, then transition to follow-up when the foot traffic begins to slow down (usually late afternoon), and then transition to whatever fun thing you're doing that night. This pattern isn't a rule. You can choose whatever pattern works best for your day. But the key is to set time in your schedule to follow up with the people you've met.

Let me reiterate an important point about follow-up. It's fairly common for students to give out contact information but then not respond to any communication. They may say they want to be invited to church, Bible study, or other events but then change their mind at the last minute. To help us navigate this changing receptivity, our ministry has a three-attempt rule, meaning, we'll only attempt to follow up a student three times. If there's no response, we'll change their receptivity color to red and stop following up.

6. Do you have any advice if we want to start developing relationships with the university faculty, staff and administrators?

It's wise to develop appropriate relationships with university faculty, staff and administrators on the campus you're reaching. After all, we all care about students and want to help them. With that in mind, our goal should be to introduce ourselves, get to know the officials, and see how we can come alongside them to serve students. The university has a lot of helpful resources for students that most ministries don't provide. Becoming familiar with those resources will better equip us to help students, as well as build trust with the university. When faculty and staff see our desire to serve, follow the campus guidelines and be a team player, it builds credibility and is a huge step toward building a long-term relationship with the university.

At the same time, we're able to help students in spiritual and practical ways that the university can't. And like any other mission field, over the years we've seen both incredible favor and opposition from the universities we reach. No matter the dynamic, our posture remains the same: to serve students and the campus community. When we can work with the university and its resources and systems, we can better help students get the help they need.

7. When you say you equip students to reach their peers, what does that look like?

Missiologists agree, locals in a community are the best people to reach their own community. That means the best people to reach college students aren't full-time campus missionaries, it's other college students. Here's how we equip our student leaders to effectively reach their peers.

Story Training

If someone asked you to share your testimony, what would you say? Would you be prepared to share how you went from spiritual death to spiritual life in a clear and engaging way? For most Christians, the answer is no. And yet sharing your story is one of the most effective ways to reach others. (That's what the Apostle Paul did all throughout the book of Acts.) That's why we train all of our student members to share their story in 2-3 minutes. We teach them to share about what their life was like before they surrendered to Jesus, how and when they surrendered to Jesus, and what their life is like now. My wife Wendy has developed a training tool to help someone write out their story so that it points others to Jesus. Half the battle is learning to communicate what God's done in your life in a clear way. (That's why we like to say, "Jesus is Lord, but clarity is king".) We believe training someone to share their own story is one of the greatest gifts you can give a young Christian.

Watch the story training here:

Engaging Students on Campus - We equip our student leaders with questions that spark conversation on campus.

Here are some examples:

- "How would you describe your current spiritual beliefs?"
- "If it turned out God was real, and you could ask any question, what would it be and why?"
- "Did you grow up with any kind of faith background? What was that like?"
- "Do you consider yourself religious or spiritual? In what way?"

Some questions are great for specific times of the school year:

- Kicking off the school year: "What are you most excited for in college?" and "What types of clubs and organizations are you looking to get involved in?"
- At the start of spring semester: "How have things been going so far in college? In what way would you want this semester to get better?"
- Leading up to Easter: "What do you think Easter is all about?"

Prayer Lists - We encourage all of our members to make a list of friends they want to reach and start praying for them. This helps focus their outreach efforts on a few specific people and, more importantly, gets them praying for their friends. We know that without the power and work of the Holy Spirit, our efforts to reach others are in vain, so we want to start with prayer and ask God for opportunities to share our story and the gospel.

Gospel Appointment Training - As I mentioned earlier, Paul and David Worcester's training on how to set up and lead Gospel Appointments has taken our ministry's evangelism to the next level.

A Gospel Appointment is simply a time to share the gospel with someone. Anyone can be trained to set up and lead a Gospel Appointment. You just need a person, a place, and a time. It doesn't matter how long you've been a Christian or how much you know about the Bible. You just have to know how to share your story and clarify the gospel (Gospelappointments.com).

There are many tools you can use to share the gospel: The Four Spiritual Laws, The God Test, The Bridge Analogy, The Roman Road, and so many others. We've developed a conversational tool on our website called The Gospel Story, and we train all of our members how to walk through this virtual tract with others.

Check out The Gospel Story:

Connect Group Leader Team - For some of our members, training them to share their story and clarify the gospel is an appropriate level of training and commitment, others want more. That's why we developed the Connect Group Leader Team. These team members receive additional training from our full-time campus missionaries to equip them to grow and lead small groups. Student leaders are trained to invite their friends from class, sports teams, and organizations to start a Bible study of eight to ten people. We've developed various Bible studies. Our *Red Book* clarifies the gospel. Our *Gray Book* helps lay a biblical foundation in students' lives. And our *Blue Book* helps students learn about finding freedom in Christ. (It's obvious that we like colors.) All of these books are designed to help students find and follow Jesus, walk in freedom, and live on mission.

Check out our website for these and other resources:

REFERENCES

Introduction

1. Luther, Martin, and Charles William Eliot. *Address to the Christian Nobility of the German Nation Respecting the Reformation of the Christian Estate*. 36, Part 5 of 6, P.F. Collier & Son, 1909, bartleby.com, https://www.bartleby.com/36/5/8.html#89, Accessed 9 Feb. 2023.
2. As of April 2023
3. Morrow, Jonathan. "Only 4 Percent of Gen Z Have a Biblical Worldview." *Impact 360 Institute*, Barna Group, 2018, https://www.impact360institute.org/articles/4-percent-gen-z-biblical-worldview/.
4. Hanson, Melanie. "College Enrollment & Student Demographic Statistics." *Education Data Initiative*, EducationData.org, 26 July 2022, https://educationdata.org/college-enrollment-statistics.
5. "Students Can Move the World." *StudentSoul*, InterVarsity, https://studentsoul.intervarsity.org/move-world.
6. As of April 2023

Chapter 1: The Battle to Belong

1. "Faculty Profile." *Faculty Profiles*, Texas State University, https://faculty.txst.edu/profile/2018070.
2. Shadrach, Steve, and Paul Worcester. *The Fuel and the Flame: Ignite Your Life & Your Campus for Jesus Christ*. Center for Mission Mobilization, 2021.
3. Cook, Halie. "First 6 Weeks of College Most Dangerous Time for Sexual Assault." 12 News, 25 Aug. 2017, https://www.12news.com/

article/news/local/arizona/first-6-weeks-of-college-most-dangerous-time-for-sexual-assault/75-467451656. Accessed 9 Feb. 2023.

4. "Shattering the Red Zone." *PAVE*, 2020, https://www.shatteringthe-silence.org/red-zone.

5. Fisher, Lauren B, et al. "From the Outside Looking In: Sense of Belonging, Depression, and Suicide Risk." *Psychiatry Interpersonal and Biological Processes*, 18 May 2015, https://www.tandfonline.com/doi/full/10.1080/00332747.2015.1015867. Accessed 9 Feb. 2023.

6. Eisenberg, Daniel, et al. The Healthy Minds Network, *The Healthy Minds Study*, https://healthymindsnetwork.org/wp-content/up-loads/2021/09/HMS_national_winter_2021.pdf. Accessed 1 Mar. 2023.

7. Department of Psychiatry and Behavioral Sciences. "The Belonging Project at Stanford." *Department of Psychiatry and Behavioral Sciences*, Stanford Medicine, 2023, https://med.stanford.edu/psychia-try/special-initiatives/belonging.html.

8. Mulvihill, Josh. "When Do Americans Become Christians?" *Gospel Shaped Family*, 13 Aug. 2018, https://gospelshapedfamily.com/dis-cipleship/when-do-americans-become-christians/.

9. As of April 2023

10. GospelAppointments.com

11. Godsnotdeadevents.org

12. As of April 2023

13. Ells, Alfred H. *The Resilient Leader: How Adversity Can Change You and Your Ministry for the Better*, David C Cook, Colorado Spring, CO, 2020, p. 192.

Chapter 2: The Fish are Still Biting

1. "About Phi Delt." *Phi Delta Theta*, Phi Delta Theta Fraternity, https://phideltatheta.org/about/.

2. Rainer, Sam. "What Two Simple Statistics Reveal about the American Church." *Sam Rainer*, 21 Jan. 2018, https://samrainer.com/2018/01/

what-two-simple-statistics-reveal-about-the-american-church/.

3. Worcester, Paul. "Summer Sessions | E18 | Give Me Freshman or Give Me Death." *Campus Ministry Today*, Center for Mission Mobilization, 20 July 2021, https://campusministry.org/podcast/give-me-freshman-or-give-me-death-by-paul-worcester.

4. Greear, J.D. "A Vision for the Centered and Sent Church." The Summit Church. Centered & Sent Conference, Durham, https://jdgreear.com/a-vision-for-the-centered-and-sent-church/. Accessed 10 Feb. 2023.

5. Stetzer, Ed. "Two Statistics Every Church Planter Needs to Know." *Outreachmagazine.com*, 24 July 2016, https://outreachmagazine.com/features/18568-two-statistics-every-church-planter-needs-to-know.html.

6. Greear, J.D. *Gaining by Losing: Why the Future Belongs to Churches That Send*. Zondervan, 2015.

7. "'The Great Commission Is Not an Option to Be Considered; It Is a Command to Be Obeyed.'." Harvest University, https://harvestuniv.org/the-great-commission-is-not-an-option-to-be-considered/.

8. "Evangelism Statistics." *Bible.org*, 2 Feb. 2009, https://bible.org/illustration/evangelism-statistics.

9. Rainer, Thom S. *The Unchurched next Door: Understanding Faith Stages as Keys to Sharing Your Faith*. Zondervan, 2003.

10. Laurenewelch. "The Stats behind 'Re-Thinking Evangelism.'" *TELLING THE GOSPEL*, 21 May 2021, https://tellingthegospel.com/2021/05/21/the-stats-behind-re-thinking-evangelism/.

11. "Fishers of Men? or Keepers of the Aquarium?" Message Ministries & Missions Inc., 8 May 2014, https://messagemissions.com/fishers-of-men-or-keepers-of-the-aquarium/.

12. One of the campus missionaries was Ken Dew, a minister with Every Nation Churches and Ministries, church planter, author of *Engaging the Culture*, and an equipping evangelist.

13. Phxgmizell. "Monty's Mantras." *NBA.com*, NBA Media Ventures, 19 May 2021, https://www.nba.com/suns/features/montys-mantras.

Chapter 3: The Strategy

1. "Prayer and Alpha." *Alpha USA*, Alpha International, https://alphausa.org/pray/.
2. Coleman, Robert E. *The Master Plan of Evangelism*. Second ed., Revell, Baker Publishing Group, 1993.
3. *Berean Study Bible*. Bible Hub, 2020, https://bible.com/bible/3034/ecc.9.10.BSB, Accessed 10 Feb. 2023.
4. "Bobsledding." *Encyclopædia Britannica*, Encyclopædia Britannica, Inc., https://www.britannica.com/sports/bobsledding.
5. Osborn, Hannah. "The Perfect Slide: The Science of Bobsledding." *STEMvisions Blog*, Smithsonian Science Education Center, 9AD, https://ssec.si.edu/stemvisions-blog/perfect-slide-science-bobsledding.
6. "Bobsleigh Info Graphics." *IBSF*, International Bobsled & Skeleton Foundation, 2015, https://www.ibsf.org/en/our-sports/bobsleigh-info-graphics.

Chapter 4: Impact Events – Breaking the Stigma on College Campuses

1. French, David. "Stigma Beats Dogma." *National Review*, 16 June 2009, https://www.nationalreview.com/phi-beta-cons/stigma-beats-dogma-david-french/. Accessed 10 Feb. 2023.
2. "A New Generation Expresses Its Skepticism and Frustration with Christianity." *Barna*, Barna Group, 21 Sept. 2007, https://www.barna.com/research/a-new-generation-expresses-its-skepticism-and-frustration-with-christianity/.
3. Camiré, Jonathan. "Bach: A Theologian at the Workplace." *The Gospel Coalition I Canada*, 4 Oct. 2020, https://ca.thegospelcoalition.org/article/bach-a-theologian-at-the-workplace/.
4. Hartropp, Joseph. "'The Divine One'? 8 Reasons Michelangelo Is The Greatest Christian Artist Of All Time." *Christian Today*, 6 Mar. 2017,

https://www.christiantoday.com/article/the-divine-one-8-reasons-michelangelo-is-the-greatest-christian-artist-of-all-time/105316.htm.

5. "The Evolution of Christian Architecture Over Time." *Russian Icon Collection*, 24 Nov. 2022, https://russianicon.com/the-evolution-of-christian-architecture-over-time/.

6. Chrzan, David, and Rick Warren. "The Importance of Evangelism for Church Growth." Rick Warren's Ministry Podcast, 14 June 2007, https://podcasts.apple.com/us/podcast/rick-warrens-ministry-podcast/id251173470. Accessed 15 Apr. 2011.

Chapter 5: Authentic Relationships – Guides Who Come Alongside

1. Elmore, Dr. Tim. "Connecting with the Emerging Generation." *IDisciple*, Growing Leaders, https://www.idisciple.org/post/connecting-with-generation-iy.

2. Batterson, Mark. *Circle Maker*. Zondervan, 2016.

3. *NLC Staff Mtg. Pastoring People Well… Known, Loved & Challenged Teaching*. 5 Feb. 2019, https://awscdn.nextlevelrelationalnetwork.com/wp-content/uploads/2019/02/23120230/Kickoff-2019-Session-3-Known-Loved-and-Challenged-Pastor-Matt-Keller-NOTES.pdf.

4. Elmore, Tim. "Five Tips for Raising Kids in a Culture of Avoidance." *Growing Leaders*, https://midvalleyfellowship.blog/2019/12/28/five-tips-for-raising-kids-in-a-culture-of-avoidance/.

5. "Chess and Checkers." *Growing Leaders*, 12 Oct. 2012, https://growingleaders.com/chess-and-checkers/. Accessed 10 Feb. 2023.

6. Maxwell, John C. *The 21 Indispensable Qualities of a Leader: Becoming the Person Others Will Want to Follow*. Thomas Nelson, 1999.

7. "Collegiate Churches and Parachurch Ministries." *Gracepoint Ministries*, 2022, https://www.gracepointonline.org/.

Chapter 6: Action Trumps Everything

1. Greear, J.D. "Four Ways to Live in Light of Heaven." *J.D. Greear Ministries*, 3 Apr. 2017, https://jdgreear.com/four-ways-to-live-in-light-of-heaven/.
2. Trainor, Tim. "How Ford's Willow Run Assembly Plant Helped Win World War II." *Assembly*, BNP Media, 3 Jan. 2019, https://www.assemblymag.com/articles/94614-how-fords-willow-run-assembly-plant-helped-win-world-war-ii.
3. Orton, Kyle W. "How Many Christians Were There in the Roman Empire?" *Kyle Orton's Blog*, 11 June 2021, https://kyleorton.co.uk/2021/06/11/how-many-christians-were-there-in-the-roman-empire/. Accessed 12 Apr. 2023.

Appendix

1. Bevere, John. *Killing Kryptonite: Destroy What Steals Your Strength*. Messenger International, Inc., 2017.
2. Shadrach, Steve. *The God Ask*. CMM Press, 2013.
3. Broocks, Rice. "Becoming an Engaging Church." *Ricebroocks.com*, The A Group, 6 May 2016, http://www.ricebroocks.com/blog/blog/. Accessed 10 Feb. 2023.

ABOUT THE AUTHOR

Brian Smith Sr. is the founding and senior pastor of Hope Church Movement, a nondenominational, collegiate-focused church planting movement reaching college campuses across the Southwest.

Brian graduated from the University of Arizona where he was a collegiate athlete and member of Phi Delta Theta Fraternity. He also served as the Interfraternity Council President and was named Greek Man of the Year. For over 35 years, he's devoted his life to helping college students find and follow Jesus, walk in freedom, and live on mission.

A native of Phoenix, Brian lives in Arizona with his wife, Wendy, their three adult sons, two daughters-in-law, and two granddaughters. He enjoys hiking, smoking meat on his Traeger grill and watching the Phoenix Suns and Arizona Cardinals. He and Wendy have been married for 32 years and are thankful to have their sons and daughters-in-law join them in full-time ministry at Hope Church Movement.

 @pastorbsmith_    @BrianSmithSr

notes

WINNING THE BATTLE TO BELONG

NOTES

WINNING THE BATTLE TO BELONG

NOTES